O U T R A G E D

ISBN 978-0-615-35061-5

ACKNOWLEDGMENTS

To my lovely wife, Dana, the best person I have ever known. To total strangers that have offered me friendly smiles and good luck wishes. Confident hand shakes, good jokes and encouragement from my co-workers and friends. To my employers who more than once gave me second chances, to my brothers, sisters, son and daughter, in-laws and outlaws, music buddies and mentors. To friends whom have past and to friends who remain. To my parents whose courage and wisdom is my sword and my shield. I remain always in your debt.

PREFACE

It doesn't take a great sense of smell to realize something is rotten on Capitol Hill. And it doesn't take a pocket full of diplomas and degrees to understand that what you once perceived as a house in order is now nothing more than an institution in chaos. Mad men and women attempting on one hand to direct and control military presence in over a hundred and thirty countries around the world, while on the other hand dictating to American business, America's health care, America's finance, intruding in American privacy. Extorting taxes from America's working men and women in order to achieve Government's own goals, breaching the constitution with reckless disregard, creating a weak and wobbly world for everyone. Not just on foreign shores and in other governments is this instability evident, but right here in America, the very place our government has lost most of its respect.

INTRODUCTION

To quote President John Fitzgerald Kennedy, "Ask not what your country can do for you, but what you can do for your country." One of the most powerful statements ever uttered. A statement that's true meaning evaded me for years but a message I will never forget, a statement that made me uncomfortable every time I heard it until I realized the profoundness of those few simple lines. This was and is a statement that carries within its meaning an awesome responsibility for anyone who would answer its challenge. A statement from someone I personally did not know has impacted my life in a way I still am unable to fully explain, but within my core has ignited a flame of indignation toward those who would destroy the beauty and the freedom for which this country ultimately stands. In front of me now lies a goal that can never fully be achieved, a journey that has no end, mountains and oceans that can never truly be conquered and overall a perpetual and awesome responsibility.

When you finish reading this book you will fully understand what I'm doing for my country. You see, right now my country is very sick and needs immediate care if it is ever going to recover. I am on a journey alongside many others that also realize a life and death battle for freedom lies just ahead. But we are ready, and with your help, we will expose and condemn, accuse and rid America of its political sham, and focus the spotlight on the corrupt maggots that have infested OUR GOVERNMENT and caused its illness. All is not lost. There is a cure. But we, all of us, must act as one body to quickly stop that which in essence would cause America's death and absolute destruction if left to the current Obama administration. The majority of those whom have caused this illness that continues to spread like cancer would sell us, (AMERICA) and what America stands for down the river if they are not stopped! You and I, and the rest of America will never see our future secure or realized fully if we do not stop at some point and start to focus our attention on what is taking place all around us. We are, and have been enslaved for years without fully recognizing it. You and I, and millions of Americans have been kept busy continually paying the piper, but we have never been allowed one dance. Our lives will be a constant struggle because we have allowed ourselves to be deceived by the very ones we've trusted to run our Government. We have stood silently by and allowed our freedom to be stolen, our privacy to be invaded, and our money to be squandered. Let's begin now by taking back what is rightfully ours. Let's dedicate ourselves and recruit others in the cause of reclaiming America and reinstating her to her rightful and honorable place.

It's time for change, but most certainly not the kind Barack Obama (BO) is talking about. For being successful, do you really want to be taxed more? I personally think that would be an incentive killer. Why would you want to work harder to support a government that wastes more? Is that equitable or even sensible? Not in my book. Whether the political arena recognizes it or not, MY OPINION MEANS SOMETHING BECAUSE I SAY SO. You are already paying for every cent of expense caused by these illegal wars we are in, and they now are attempting to impose a war tax on you? Would you like to look at your check at the end of the week and realize nothing has been stolen from you in the form of tax? And all the money that you earned is yours. That tax refund check at the end of the year is a joke, and a bad one at that. Simply put, it is nothing more than a smoke screen. Don't you see the scam? They have to make it look like they're giving you something in order to continue taking from you. Have you forgotten the thousands of dollars you paid over the years to an illegal agency called the IRS along with the hundreds of millions and billions of dollars that Congress and the Federal Reserve has stolen from you through deceptive maneuvering and manipulation of America's finances? That is theft by deception, and it carries a penalty of imprisonment. If you for one moment think that anyone in Washington, D.C. gives a damn about you or what you think, then it's time for you to open your eyes to the reality of what is taking place and has been ever since the politicians and the bankers got together back in the 1900's and realized they could combine forces and rob us at will if a tax system was part of the Federal Reserve scheme. When the Congress became the legal partners with the Federal Reserve, you became a permanent victim. You think the stimulus packages of late are something new? Every time there has been a financial crisis in this country of major financial institutions, manufacturing companies, corporations, railroads, airlines, etc., government has taken your tax money and bailed those institutions out, thereby keeping you and the rest of America enslaved. That is communism. There are literally hundreds of billions of dollars lifted from the pockets of the unsuspecting tax payer and no one is any the wiser. Don't feel bad, the majority of Americans still don't get it. But now that you do, that should make you mad as hell. Not only in America is this happening, it's happening all around the world. Europe is paying approximately eight dollars per gallon or more for its gasoline, at the time of this writing, and half of that is tax. Still the Queen and her ROYAL subjects lavishly entertain and enjoy a superior lifestyle while all the time there is an element of every society that has no shelter, no food, no jobs, and no one to guide or educate them. Where is all that tax money going? The world will soon be approaching an emotional meltdown, and a tremendous explosion of emotions will certainly take place. Cash for clunkers is not a new idea. We will have cash for clunkers as long as we continue supporting our present type of government. Keep reading and never give up your guns!!! The time has come to hold government responsible and

MAKE them stay the course of responsibility when it comes to taking our money. We will simply have to take the money away from them, disconnect and eliminate the Federal Reserve System. By doing so, the Federal Reserve System can no longer counterfeit our currency. As a people we have been deceived by the very ones whom we have entrusted. There is a term in civil matters called theft by deception, and that simply means that someone lies to you to get your money or property, etc. The Supreme Court and our constitution states very clearly that our income tax is voluntary. Therefore, no demand for such payment can be made, nor seizures threatened for non-voluntary payment, but Government has invoked a dictatorship in this particular part of the constitution because it serves them, NOT YOU. To quote President Ronald Reagan, the most feared nine words you will ever hear is, 'I'm from the government, and I'm here to help'. They are here to help themselves to your money and whatever else they can steal is what that means. Help - so they can bail out the losers with your money. Other peoples' business and/or failure, that you had nothing to do with and therefore, certainly isn't your responsibility. They are here to help drive you so far into debt that it will steal your children's future!!!

I have heard people complain for years about the abuse of the IRS and the injustice to the American taxpayer, but no one ever does anything about it because they feel helpless or afraid that they would be singled out for making waves. But you've got to understand as long as you look the other way or refuse to organize, your efforts will surely fail. This is a new day, and the world is rapidly approaching a showdown. We have instant information and disbursement and distribution via specific technology that can alert the world in an instant if necessary. Also, there is instant communication including new and better ways to control or demand from government more responsibility on their part. It is OUR money that runs everything from business to churches to charities to hospitals to Governments. And there is only one way to control such a wasteful Government. We simply have to withhold the money that government loves to waste so well. We as a society have to hold government responsible to us. I don't know of any business that allows the workers to control the purse strings do you? Then why do we, the employer, even consider allowing the employee, OUR

GOVERNMENT, to control the checkbook? Do you see what I mean? You will as we continue. We have given this government free reign to spend and waste at will! And then they tell us; their employer, that we have to cough up another $500 million because Congress wants some new airplanes. And, so shortly after they just condemned the auto manufacturers for flying to Washington, D.C. in private planes!! At least the auto executives paid for their own planes out of the fruits of their own labor. I had much rather pay for the auto manufacturer than big mouth Presidents, Congressmen and women that have NEVER produced anything but trouble, waste and confusion. The auto manufacturer at least, has produced for many years, something positive and useful for generations that which has benefited people around the world. While governments have produced nothing but CONFUSION, WARS, AND DEBT - Inexcusable Debt!!!

So that everybody including government has money to function, we have to start to think what is honorable. We have to eliminate the IRS as it is today and move toward something more palatable for the American people and this nation. I heard the former president of the

United States, President George W. Bush, if you can call him a President, make a statement that he knows why the rich are taxed differently than the rest of the citizens of the United States, and that is because they can afford attorneys to find loopholes in the tax system and avoid paying tax like the rest of the Americans. I thought how stupid, how arrogant, and how unfair! If the loopholes are there, then why is it that not all Americans are privileged to them? The whole idea of an IRS is a sham and a scam anyway. The IRS system is outright thievery and ILLEGAL - PERIOD!!! The idea here is not to avoid our responsibility to our country, but for everyone to support, control, and demand the government be operated fairly and honestly – as long as we have a government that is fairly regulated and controlled. What is wrong with the idea of everyone supporting the country according to their personal lifestyle choice? Or, do we just let the government inflate the currency when they are too afraid to impose further taxation. It's what they have been doing for years when they, the government, don't have the guts to face the taxpayer with another tax increase. None of this tax crap needs to exist. That is clearly stated in the sixteenth amendment. None of us has to even fill out any paper work for the thieves at the IRS. We all live in this country and enjoy its freedoms and opportunities. No one class has the right to control or diminish another class or control the other class by taxing them differently than the other, or taxing them at all. Some have suggested a flat tax or consumer tax of 15%. OK, that is still far more generous than they deserve any way. Why would you reward a thief in any amount? Who would be able to escape paying their fair share, if there is a fair share that anyone owes anyway? I'm actually being more generous with that statement than I should be by even stating it this way. The tax, according to the constitution, is only to be delivered by corporations. A tax derived from those profits. Not by the working men and women. Not by the laborers. So, don't be afraid to speak out and become active in eliminating an unfair system. Fear keeps you small and helpless and non-productive in your efforts. And they, the IRS, know that. You, therefore remain the victim and are easily defeated when this happens. These statements and ideas are in no way intended to overthrow our government or the system or cause chaos, but to bring our government into compliance and under the people's rightful and reasonable control. It is government that needs to be controlled. It is Government that has to be controlled. It is 2/10/10, and our Nation's economy is suffering terribly because we have not controlled our Government. It is our fault for not holding a tight line on these losers. Government must be responsible to the people who support and move government forward with the very money people pay to government's coffers. I don't waste my money, and I sure as hell have no intention of giving it to this undeserving government to waste for me. My intention is to eliminate the wasteful ways for which government is so famous. Eliminate them by removing their abusive powers. Remember the money that our government wastes is not theirs to waste. I don't care how you cut it; Government has to be responsible with OUR MONEY. If this government were of the private sector, they would all be imprisoned for conspiracy to defraud the American people, charged with reckless disregard, misappropriation of funds and embezzlement, including counterfeiting. Let's take away that power when it comes to our money NOW! That's the only thing that gives them power anyway. They sure as hell are not some brand of super human or anything else. But that's what they want you to believe. That certainly should not be hard for anyone to figure out. They have bullied their way into our lives and we have allowed them to rob us while making us believe they are worthy of their power. They are not in control!!! But because we as Americans don't know what our own constitution says, how the hell do we expect to stay out in front of our own stupidity? You've heard the phrase, 'knowledge is power'. Well you see it in action every time the fucking IRS raises its ugly head.

This loose handed responsibility by our officials is not acceptable! And, if it means taking drastic measures to show them that we the American people mean business then we will have to get the process started! But it's going to take all of us. There needs to be a groundswell of opposition legally and orderly, but not however according to their standard. It needs to be organized according to our demands and you need to be a part of it. You will find forms in the back of this book to direct you in the proper ways of supporting this effort. My whole point is to make changes in a positive and productive way for all Americans and start the recovery process of this great nation. The only way that happens is for everyone, rich, poor, young and old alike, to be treated equally under a well planned, deliverable system. Something you will never get under the BO or any other traditional political system or administration. Since you will be paying the tax on whatever may be the lifestyle you choose to live, you will at least be in control of your destiny, not some leach that thinks he/she has the right to your money. If you want to drive an exotic car and live in a two million dollar condo, great! Just pay the tax on your purchase. That's simple enough to understand. There would be no tax forms to fill out, no reason for the hundreds of millions of dollars spent on overhead and salaries for those despicable human Dobermans that know only how to inflict pain, suffering and fear on the unfortunate, or those whom have fallen victim to believing such fallacies that the IRS has the right to confiscate property and destroy lives and families with intimidation and threats of imprisonment because people refuse to pay a part of their money to those who have the morals of pigs. These people are in for a rude awakening. It's robbery, and robbery is illegal in every language. But then again the IRS is illegal and has been operating illegally ever since the government failed to ratify the 16th amendment…PROVE ME WRONG! SHOW ME THE LAW!

If anyone should be imprisoned, it should be all of the losers who ever had anything to do with harming an American citizen for failure to pay to a tax system that we now all know is illegal. Terrorism comes in all forms and happens in many places. Not just somewhere outside our country, but sometimes right under your nose - sometimes by our own trusted government. That's reason enough alone to maintain the right to bear arms! Please, get as rich as you can dream and become what you are supposed to be without fear of being robbed by your own government. Then you will know what it really means to truly be a free American. We the people have always been out in front of the government on everything that happens. Don't get me wrong, we need a government. But we need one that serves the will of the people, not one that is self-serving, not one that has a voracious appetite for everything belonging to everyone else, and at the expense of the very people that keep government functioning - not the pathetic likes of the Clintons, Ted Kennedy, the Bushes, and now the BO's. How sick do we have to become before we regurgitate this kind of poison and remember never again to allow this kind of embarrassment to represent the American people ever again be it Democrat Republican or independent! We have to have a government where no one is above the law and everyone is accountable for their actions. We don't need a tax collection system. We need a tax support system (maybe). We need a different system altogether, but we're going to need a system that is privatized, not one controlled by government. American people need to know and control where their money is being used, such as allowing the people to view open books. The people need a government that is also accessible without having to know somebody in high places. Ask yourself if you know where any of the money has gone that you paid in taxes in any given year. What would you say? Schools, roads, police departments, fire departments, etc. If you're like most Americans, you're just handing your money over and probably saying what's the use, my voice doesn't make any difference. Well, think of something that would make a difference if your voice was heard. Would you like to have another $500 in your pocket each month, or maybe a $1,000 or more? What if you looked at the deductions in your weekly check and there were none! Why don't you look at all these things that you could do with that extra money instead of giving it to some agency that has been robbing you blind along with all the rest of America for as long as you have been in the workforce? What a relief to know you don't have to fill out those tax forms at the end of every year just to satisfy some evil, greedy, thieving con men and women controlling the IRS. Ever try to get government to give you anything without trying to control every aspect of your life? Government doesn't give you anything! Government only takes from you, and they will continue to take from you as long as you will cave in. The only time that you will get noticed is when you start to make some noise. Remember the Million Man March on Washington? Do you remember what it accomplished? Neither do I. It was a waste of time and money and had no real impact on anything. If the resources from that kind of action and other non-impact stunts went into legally forcing the Congress to come to the negotiating table through legal avenues and processes you would be seeing a change already and you wouldn't have the absolute garbage you have in government today. You saw how the government responded to the victims of the hurricanes that hit the coast of Mississippi, Alabama, and Louisiana? Those people are all taxpaying Americans! Should there not have been as much news coverage and condemnation from everyone toward the lack of response from FEMA and other flimsy, irresponsible, government bodies there still wouldn't be as much done to help those people. If the state of Texas hadn't had the warning that it had, that of course would be a different story. Do I need to say any more? Just because it is the state where the former president calls home... Ooh, don't misread what I mean by saying it's where the former president calls home. The president wouldn't have anything to do with it, but the response would be automatic. Get my point? The former president had his hands full just pretending to run this country along with an illegal war that he started including an out of control economy, it also is just that he was surrounded with total and utter incompetence. You know, like attracts like, which shows his ultimate level of competence! It seems that no one actually knows who is in control. Wasting hundreds of millions and billions of dollars just to pay the interest on our national debt is a

STUPID AND WASTEFUL maneuver by the STUPID AND WASTEFUL PEOPLE we have in control. Do you realize this current government is spending $1.4 billion dollars per day in interest alone at the time of this writing? That's your money! THAT'S YOUR MONEY!! THAT'S YOUR MONEY PEOPLE!!! That's $511 billion dollars per year that we're giving away to those who hold our debt. We are arming our enemies, and I believe it is intentional. What kind of leadership do you call that? Do you realize we're paying people salaries to waste our taxes, and no one in government can or will stop this? This is absolute insanity, but just another example of the level of total stupidity and incompetence in our government. This has to come to a screeching halt. There are kindergarten students that know exactly what to do when this kind of an emergency alarm sounds. You do not hesitate to go into full alert and full response when there is an emergency of this magnitude. What we have to do as Americans is bring our government back from this state of insanity and disregard for our rights and our money. We have plenty of organizations that could use that kind of money right here in the United States, not ACORN though, please!!!

We must demand, and I'm not talking about pretty please here. I said DEMAND spending as we go and reign in these suicidal idiots. What an embarrassment to this country and to the American people. What a waste of the people's money and what mistrust is generated out of such disasters. Our government has to at some point be responsible to us, and that time is right fucking now!!! We elect these numb-nuts to run the country responsibly, NOT RUN US INTO RUIN!!! What we have right now is a lazy, sick, bloated, embarrassing scum-bag government, and we have to get rid of the parasites that have so easily inhabited it! The taxpayer/American businessman and women/families and individuals are required by law to balance their books every year, yet this government never balances its books! In fact, it keeps a different set of books than other businesses and this government has an altogether different form of accounting - the very thing that sends people to jail in the private sector. Every new administration promises to balance the budget yet we end up more in debt than the last administration. This is criminal and a continual lying promise that every administration makes to the American people. The lies and deception will never be rectified because we the people are cowards. We are passive and we are under the influence of false respect. We have become like silly little groupies at a concert, not realizing that these empty suits are our undermining enemies. The con men and women in our government have attempted to seduce us through this doctrine of 'father knows best' bull shit, and they're not about to stop any time soon. They are the Jim Joneses and we have been drinking their poison in more and more delusional doses. We cannot allow this government to continue to insult us while they rob us of not only our freedom but our dignity, money, and our constitutional heritage. We cannot allow this government to continue to stack up the debt that will eventually consume the entire tax base just to pay the interest on that debt. When that becomes the case, what happens then? There will be no money for law enforcement, there will be no money for fire departments, there will be no money for schools, there will be no money for highways, and there will be no money for homeland security. There will be no money for anything but paying the interest on the debt that we still have in the trillions of dollars! What happens then, we turn this country over to the foreign nations that hold our debt? Well, we are on the verge of that very thing right now. America, the richest country in the world is broke because of whom we have elected and allowed to destroy OUR great nation! That's what we can look forward to if we do not take this country now and shake loose all of the parasites that have only their own interest in mind. We must at all costs be cautious of the people we elect or allow to remain in office. We need those in office whom have a realistic sense of duty to this great nation and not to the benefactor of self. They must realize that prosperity automatically will come to those who are of character and of substance. But, we the people must educate ourselves about who we put in charge and we have to be bold enough to take charge of what we know to be out of step with the American greatness or we will lose what little amount of respect we have left from the rest of the world. It is time to do some much needed and overdue renovation, starting with the White House and all the greedy little parasites that have for too long inhabited the great house of OUR nation. There are value producers and there are value destroyers, and I don't have to point out or explain to you what I mean by my statements regarding the dysfunctional state of our government. You know what I mean. You know the corruption and phony egos and wasteful indignant irresponsible transparent garbage I'm talking about. Deceiving the American people has become a way of life for those people. They know from past experience we will do nothing like we have done in the past. It is time to write a new page in history. It is time for you and me to get down to business. Our opposition has been tirelessly working behind the scenes to reduce America and what we stand for to ashes and to bring this country to a third world status. We have to stop right here and right now to reverse this trend and bring about a change that will put us back on track and head us in the right and honorable direction. However; the people that we elect will have to realize that they will either take the bows for a job well done, or feel the sting from the fiery darts of criticism. Whatever the case may be, it will ultimately be a direct result of the stance WE take as the citizens of America, and I mean all of us - red, yellow, brown, black and white. Without the American people and the contributions we make to this government, what is there? If you stop to think seriously about who is in charge or who is in control, you would be seriously amazed. Listen, we do not need their permission, so don't get caught behind that thought. Thinking that we need someone's permission to raise all holy hell is not the way to think at all. Look, governments are the perfect place for crooks to congregate. Maggots all look alike and all act alike and are all there for one reason, and that is to take everything you have, starting with your money. Our money is the only reason we have what we have on Capitol Hill and nothing more. We must have a transfusion of fresh blood, fresh minds and legitimate integrity. We, at all cost, must have committed people who love America and care what happens by protecting her greatness. Not what we have presently. Not those who inhabit America's greatness for a free ride to a dead end, but those who have vision, those who have lasting character. Not those that once have had their fill and abandon what we stand for. I think I can safely say just before you see the last one of the Bush or BO administration go over the horizon, you can bet the last thing that they voted on was to give themselves a raise! We have elements and departments of this government that are deadly to the existence and survival of all of us. We have been somehow living with this disease for as long as I can remember. But now, at all cost, we must reclaim, by revolution if necessary, what is rightfully a gift to all of us from our founding fathers who paid the ultimate price so that we, their descendents, could live in unencumbered freedom with a constitution and bill of rights specifically designed and developed for all of us as an ultimate guarantee of those freedoms and protection from an oppressive Government.

The tax system, the banking system, and the Federal Reserve were the primary cause of the Great Depression, and consequently, every financial crisis this country has ever faced since has been due to manipulation of the financial systems and or financial disruption "caused" intentionally by those whom we have ALLOWED to stay in control. What fool can't see what needs to be done? The IRS is absolute poison to you and your financial future or any other future you may envision. It is organized terrorism and hell bent on robbing you of any chance you have at financial freedom. The IRS code has over 9 million words in it and even those who wrote it don't understand it, and also can't explain it. And yet, this government is too greedy, to blind, stupid, or too fucking lazy to want to change it for the better or incorporate a new fair and equitable plan. But why should they? YOU ARE NOT THEIR CONCERN. It has served them well. They can rob us at will. We are the people that have to take back control. No one is going to volunteer to do this for us. But I will guarantee you, what we have in control now are not the people we want running this country. These are not the people we want running even for dog catcher! Come on people, we as Americans despise governments that take advantage of its citizens. The reason America is America is because we refused to be taxed unfairly in the past, and we had a tea party and told GRAND OLE' England where to stick it with their excessive tax. As an act of defiance we threw all their tea in the God damned harbor - end of story. A new nation called America sprang to life! And another new America will spring to life when, WE THE PEOPLE get sick enough to do something about this absolute repulsive heap of stinking bullshit we have on Capitol Hill.

We go to great lengths to rescue other people from oppressive governments. We fight wars to free other nations from dictators and self-imposed tyrants. Yet we do nothing to protect ourselves or our children from such as we have here in America. Every time you turn around there's something that the government has done that infuriate most of us, case in point. The Supreme Court's passage of the law regarding eminent domain that allows confiscation of property owned by a private party, and giving that property to a corporation or another private party that would develop a larger tax base for the government's voracious appetite for anything that has money attached to it. Or better yet, take everything you own, and then send you on your merry little way like a red-headed step child.

When you finish reading this book, you need to pick up a copy of "Men in Black" by Mark R. Levin, published by Regnery Publishing. Also pick up a copy of the "Flat Tax Revolution by Steve Forbes, also published by Regnery. Both of these books break it down so no one has a problem understanding what fools the American people have been by not taking control of this government a long time ago, as well as show you what different tax systems in other parts of the world have in common. The more you read and start to understand, the clearer the picture becomes. We the American taxpayers are constantly intimidated and controlled like dangling puppets dancing on the end of a string, subjected to all of the controls that are imposed on us by the very people we elect to run this government. The thing that is most frustrating to me and millions of others I'm sure is, what is the purpose of a government who wants to harm the very people that put them in place? The very people that support that government's function are at the end of the whip, so to speak. Why would anyone want to impose hardship on the very people who would give you your job? Are they so blind and greedy, or is there in every human the trigger that causes this vagarious reaction once they have attained their goals? Do we all develop this tyrannical mentality once we have attained our desired position or goal? Stop and think just for a moment, why is it that the government does not want you to have any form of control? Why is it that the government keeps putting roadblocks in front of your progress? What possible reason does government have to continue burdening the people through oppression? Past history has proven time and time again that the less tax imposed on the citizens, the more productive everyone becomes, thus the more government is also able to make. It's simple; the economy surges forward, the people become more successful due to a thriving plentiful upsurge in trading while spending more. The circle becomes complete with less disruption, and the market finds its own equilibrium and eventually, self balances.

The picture is very clear to me at least. Unreasonable politicians and tyrants need to be removed and reeducated with a swift kick in the ass, for they are, and have always been about control. This idea of politicians who are nonproductive, stagnant, lame, dead weight, and overall in everybody else's way, live only to deprive others of any success and seem only to be focused and determined to be counter productive overall to our, or any progressive government, society, and or economy. The tax system of today is a direct result of no one taking action or doing anything to stop government's progression. We as Americans went from a no tax system in the 1800's to what we have today simply because the American population of that era leading all the way up the present time has done nothing to stop the IRS's malignant growth. Like cancer, it grows and spreads. If we've learned anything from history at all, it is to be able to recognize and to understand that when the sharks smell blood, they're going to do everything in their power to attack and devour whatever is in the immediate area! The answer is simple, never negotiate where they, the enemy, has any chance of success on any level. Because as we have seen, once those relentless dogs get their noses under the tent they're going to find a way in if there is any food to be found. The facts are clear, and history has been written. These people are not public servants. They are public parasites. You tell me, what's wrong with stopping the thief before he robs you? It is simple, and it is common sense and simple logic - be prepared on all fronts. I have seen this kind of underhanded trickery and deceptive maneuvering in the corporate world whereby a business is absorbed by whatever means and stripped of all its assets before arriving at the point of filing bankruptcy and allowing total collapse with no possibility of recovery. You had better watch BO and his minions because what is in charge of this country now is the blind leading the blind and they're picking up speed because they know we are onto them.

Saddam Hussein could have gone down in history as a prince among men. He controlled a nation that was rich in oil and even though his position was self imposed he lacked compassion, his appetite for power and control made him a target. He was a disgustingly hated man that destroyed people's lives and invaded his neighbors in an attempt to gain more through greed. The same is seen in what we have in our government today. Like Mussolini, Hitler, Pol Pot and all that tried to destroy and control others through greed and unnecessary means in the end lost their own lives as a result. So, as you can clearly see, and as all political outlaws will eventually realize, the people will only be governed so far, and robbed of so much, and taxed of so much. I'm suggesting that this government take the pulse of this nation and ready themselves as a body to do the right thing by the very oath they have taken.

What cannot be changed, and what will not be changed is that the people of this nation will not under any circumstance be enslaved by an oppressive government. American soldiers have given their lives to preserve freedom for not only this nation but for other people and other nations, and willingly so. We are not asleep! In fact, we are wide awake more than ever before, and we're telling this government that enough is enough! The fabric of patience with you has worn thin. It is time you, whom we have elected, run this country properly, run this country in a productive manner to benefit all Americans. Not in the manner that you turn on the American people in an attempt to make them your beasts of burden.

You have separated yourselves from the people to whom you are responsible, the very people you owe for the position you hold. You have taken the stance and the position that the people are your subjects and that you can dictate what is and has long been counterproductive to America's wishes. Not so!

Let's look at the Constitution, our Constitution. Not their Constitution, the Constitution of the United States of America. The Constitution belongs to all Americans, not to those who are trying to change its meaning and its wording to suit only government's agenda. The preamble of the Constitution states clearly that the authority rests with the people and not the government! Now, go to the Declaration of Independence and read very clearly that "all persons are created equal with certain unalienable rights and that governments derive their power from the consent of the governed". Hear me now! Let this sink in. Governments derive their power from the consent of the governed. Any question? That's very clear to me - very clear indeed!

Now, we elect these people and they become our enemies attempting to enslave us with their distorted view of the position with which we have just given and entrusted them. Common sense tells me that when you live in such a garbage dump as do many of our elected, it's hard to recognize just how filthy you have become! However, once you step outside of the picture and turn around to see with what you have been associated, and what you have become, you can start to get your vision back, if you don't commit suicide first. Great men and women have overcome their addiction to power and the control that grips their lives and eventually destroys them as well as their families and friends. But that regret and memory are their constant companions and forever accompany them as reminders never to return to the past for anything ever again. This feeding frenzy on the American taxpayer's money and constitutional rights has become so addictive that it is doubtful we will ever find a champion of the American people in an elected official.

The framers of the Constitution and the Bill of Rights had no fear of what oppressive authority might think or say. We the American people have begun to realize that history is repeating itself and we have recognized too, there is another tea party in the making. But this time these parasites live among us and are easily recognized and more accessible than you might think.

I awoke this morning at 5:00 a.m. clear minded, purposeful and focused. It is my wife's birthday, and it felt special to me as well. So without hesitation I removed myself from bed, shut off the alarm so that it wouldn't disturb her further. Normally I prepare something small for breakfast, have a cup of coffee and then proceed to the garage for a pretty intense workout for about a half-hour to 45 minutes. But this morning, I went straight to my office and started to research and write more on this book. I realized suddenly that there are hundreds of millions of people in all walks of life that get up every morning just like me and start their continuing journey through life. Numerous people not giving much thought to their lives and the contributions they make to their country and community, but quietly accept being robbed in small amounts, nickels and dimes, and dollars at a time. Now stop to visualize the thousands of little streams of money flowing to the IRS from all over the country. These little streams of your tax money turn into rivers of money, and by the time they reach the government waste camps, it is astonishing, the mountains of money arriving on a daily basis. So, with excess in such amounts, it's no wonder they think they have hit the mother load and your money is there for whatever reason they want to spend it on. And believe me they're not going to give that money up so easily. They are addicted to your money, and you're going to have to fight, literally, to keep from being robbed of your own finances by these swollen heads that believe you will never do anything but talk and complain. In a lot of ways they are right. It's our fault for not stopping this kind of illegal activity before now. We have money addicts on our hands, and if you know anything about addiction, you must realize this will be intense. Not everyone realizes just how much control government has on their lives. Every person in the U.S. who has a retail business works for the IRS to some degree, collecting tax without compensation. That's crap! You are slave labor, living under the threat of an oppressive government agency, and an illegal one! But we consider collecting sales tax and making timely payments to the IRS part of the price we pay for doing business.

America needs to unite NOW, and inform Washington that it will accept nothing less than the flat tax system and nothing less than what its Citizens demand. Get your hands off our money and out of our lives with your continuous deception and blatant lying for your own good. There is nothing unpatriotic about telling the IRS or any other corrupt government official, TO DROP DEAD and that you have no intention of letting them get away with robbing you of anything ever again! In essence, we as Americans are preparing for war on an enemy that we are very familiar with, but also, one that we have surrounded, and one that cannot escape our furor. We don't have leaders and representatives of the people in this country anymore. We have parasites in suits and dresses that come to the forums for a slap on the back and a free lunch, congratulating each other like they've been nominated for some great

34

achievement. I would rather honor the working men and women and give the award to the trucker who always delivers the goods. You don't see the secretaries of the country being hailed as heroes, but if you would stop and think for a minute, most companies would fall apart if the secretaries and office personnel stopped functioning.

You would see everything come to a sudden stop if we as Americans shouted loud enough so the deaf in Washington who think they are untouchable heard the word INDICTMENT! There is no accepting anything less than what the owners of this country demand from the people who work for us. Once we start to think in this manner we will get something accomplished. As I stated earlier, this book is not intended to create chaos, but to get the attention of you the reader, and to resurrect the authority that we as a people constitutionally have over abusive elected officials that have for too long gotten away with murder. We the people have failed each other because we have failed to do anything about this injustice. Being an elected official means nothing to me if you are a crook! Being an elected official means nothing to me if you're not there to dig in and represent the people who elected you. Being an elected official means nothing to me if you have promised in your campaign speeches that you would eradicate the corruption and abuses of government or special interests, and unless you keep your word and your promises that got you elected, then you have become an enemy of the people and you have become a bloodsucker just like the bloodsuckers that have caused the pain and suffering and hardship that will forever echo in your quiet moments of self reflection. Traitor! Traitor! Traitor!

I suppose that the first thing we should do to start would be to shame those who have attempted to deceive us and laugh at them and point our finger at them and undress them of their egos and hidden agendas - make fun of them for their attempt to take advantage of their fellow Americans. But let us also remind them that we the American people will hold them accountable for their actions, and that the price they pay will far exceed a slap on the wrist!

We take drunken drivers off the streets and prosecute them for driving under the influence. We take drunken pilots out of the air and prosecute them for flying an aircraft while intoxicated and endangering the lives of the passengers. Well, there is a court that we the American people control, a court that has no bureaucracy. It has no pork, it has no reason for existence other than to fulfill the wishes of the American people and it only requires us to state our dissatisfaction with leadership gone awry. This court of public opinion speaks loud, and it speaks clear. But it takes all of us to come together with a force well-prepared to do battle. This is the court of public opinion. It is the people's court, and it is there to protect and serve you and me. On the television show Hannity and Colmes, in October 2005, they spoke of an Ohio woman who was arrested and jailed for allegedly owing the IRS $1.16 – one dollar and sixteen cents. Now, according to Steve Forbes' book, "Flat Tax Revolution", on page 68, corporations avoid more than $18 billion in tax because of the lopsided unfair tax code. Need I say more? And these thugs in the IRS are operating out in the open and will continue getting away with it if WE do nothing about it. G. Gordon Liddy once said on his radio broadcast, "if they come to your door, aim for the head". How did we sleep through this? How did we allow this rogue department to get away with this kind of treatment of the

American people? We can thank Congress for the Ways and Means committee and the 'Injustice' Department for being so quick to kiss everybody's ass on Capitol Hill in an attempt to enslave America. We can also thank ourselves for not stopping every illegal move the IRS has made with the blessings of our beloved Congress, right Charlie Rangel? These bloodsuckers are the very people that we have entrusted with our welfare. Everything that has been done to this point has not worked to relieve the tax burden on the American citizen. Promises made of tax cuts here and there, while they add double someplace else, are a game they have learned to play well. They really think that we are stupid and that we will do nothing but talk and complain. I know other writers that would take a different approach to stating facts regarding the problems we face in America with what they see as out of control government. But I want to relate to your frustrations and true feelings because that's the only way to get under your skin and move you as I'm moved. To hope you feel what I feel. To let you know what I know. To bring us together, to get up and do something about the problems we face. WE HAVE ALLOWED SOMEONE ELSE TO THINK FOR US FOR

TOO LONG! You see what happens when you let the government assume control of your life instead of you having control of government? It's like spilling a drop of mercury. It spreads in a thousand directions and is instantly unmanageable. It fails to serve its original purpose and when you finally contain it, you're always wondering if you got it all because it is deadly poisonous if or when used improperly. You need to pick up a book by David Cay Johnston titled "Perfectly Legal". It will awaken you to the absolute decay we have in this government and the outright thieves with whom we are dealing. Thanks to Charlie Rangel and his minions, the government now has the idea that your tax money is theirs! And, they believe they can take your money without permission to bail out private enterprise. The BUSH and OBAMA administrations have become more ruthless and more deceptive than Enron, and yet, out of minimum wage in part, comes the automatic raises Congress loves to give itself. And still, they sell their office for private gain to the lobbyist with the most money because they just can't get enough, right William Jefferson? We have deadly enemies of the people working within our government. America and what it stands for can and will only survive if it becomes protected by the people. The world's population, still see America as a shining beacon of hope, a land of the free, where the oppressed can start a new life and raise their families in a free and responsible caring society. I have talked to people from all over this world and the story is the same. GOVERNMENTS WANT IT ALL. You and I are the only ones that can reverse this trend, and we have to start by getting rid of the problem itself. Replace the IRS with accountants, and the tax collection, if even needed at that point, would be applied at the POINT OF SALE. THERE IS AN INSTANT FIFTY BILLION DOLLAR SAVINGS to start. It remains however, that this government is for sale to anyone that has money to contribute to this political sewer. The transparency can be seen in all forms of campaigning. The American people have lost confidence in the government, and with good reason. The reason that the IRS and Congress will fight the flat tax is that they know if it ever succeeds, they can no longer steal from you. They have robbed Americans of their homes, finances, freedoms and rights. And, they have imprisoned numerous innocent people - not legally of course, but to instill fear in you, to suppress you. In some cases, some victims have committed suicide. But you must realize that if the IRS is ever found guilty in a court of law it will have to repay all that it has stolen in the form of taxation, and that is too much to even imagine. The law suits brought against government would stack a thousand miles high. Go now to http://www.originalintent.org/commentaries/wt phearing.php.

This nation needs to rise up now and demand from the government that government is to protect this country from all enemies foreign and domestic as stated in the taking their oath of office. The facts are in front of us, and what we must do now is start taking back what we have allowed to escape our control. We are so accustomed to being told what to do it seems we have lost the initiative to form our own thoughts. When it comes to having any freedom in this country, self rule is a heavy load and an awesome responsibility. But then we are responsible people. History has proven that we are hard working and committed to a better life for everyone. But here is the bottom line - the government has no respect for you and me, regardless. If they did have, you wouldn't be reading this book. You wouldn't be treated like you are. Your voice would not be lost in the wind. There would be solutions made and brought about to end this inequality. There would be no political correctness and there would be no racism. There would be no wars. People do not start wars. Let this resonate loud and clear with you. Governments, tyrants, and dictators start wars, and then expect you to fight them. They call you patriots when you do fight, so you will have a feel-good feeling about the horrible acts you are committing. But they will call you traitors and attempt to prosecute you if you don't fight. As they lay your sons, and daughters, mothers and fathers in the dust, they revel in their power and gloat in the taking of lives by the millions as history has most certainly proven. Using our tax money to accomplish their bloody tasks makes all of us accessories to their crimes. We need to purge our government of all this corruption and of all the crooked politicians that come to the table to hoist their glasses in celebration of their bloodthirsty accomplishments. Our tax money has become their blood money. They have taken refuge and positioned themselves above you and me, and above the law itself; protecting and insulating themselves by the very laws they write. What cowards, and how disgusting are these lower-than-life murderous parasites.

Ted Kennedy, even after leaving an innocent woman to drown in an accident remained in politics until his death. Acting and criticizing others like he was some authority on the moral mission. When in all reality, he, like the Clintons, Bushes and Obamas, have lived lavishly on public assistance all their political lives - TAX MONEY. Let's also not forget Janet Reno, who murdered numerous innocent people at Waco, Texas. Regardless of some religious leader's stance on what he believed or taught, those innocent lives, those children, were not collateral and without meaning. Those lives were to be protected and saved if possible. And believe me, it was possible. There are numerous accounts of those innocent of any crime, being shot by federal agents while trying to escape the fiery compound during that murderous engagement. For more information, do an internet search for "Janet Reno, David Koresh, Waco, Texas". Every direction you look, you see something happening that identifies the heavy oppressive hand of government. There is also an underlying conspiracy going on in this country that former president George Bush, the president of Mexico, and the head of Canada are in it up to their eyeballs, and that is why there is no closing the borders between Mexico, Canada, and the United States. The borders between the United States and Mexico are not going to be closed any time soon, and the borders between Canada and the United States are not going to be closed any time soon either. There is a reason! Unless we shake the elected loose from their strangle hold on America and the intrusion on the rest of the world, we will continue experiencing attacks on our rights and the continued loss of our freedoms. This country and its citizens will remain in danger of our own government terrorist aggression.

Congressman Ron Paul calls it blow back from the intrusion and actions we have taken in the past. Here are a few incidents and a matter of public record that you will remember. We will start with the assignation of Bobby Kennedy. In 1993, the World Trade Center was bombed the first time. In 1972, Munich Olympic athletes were kidnapped and murdered. The U.S. Embassies were invaded and taken over. In the 1980's, Americans were kidnapped in Lebanon. In 1985, a cruise ship was pirated, and one handicapped passenger was murdered and thrown overboard. I remember that vividly as it was shown over and over on national television. In 1985, a TWA flight was hijacked, and one person died trying to rescue the hostages. In 1988, Pan Am flight #103 was bombed. In 1998, US Embassies in Kenya and Tanzania were also bombed. On 9/11/01, the World Trade Center towers were attacked, and four jet airplanes were hijacked and crashed in various locations in the U.S. The U.S. fought a war in Afghanistan in 2002. And, just so you will know, all of this activity involved in some way, Muslim male extremists. Is that profiling or all just a coincidence? Well, I don't give a rat's ass what you want to call it. I'm using it as an example to show these politically correct numb-nuts what it really is. As if they don't already know…

And to that, I could give a shit what my critics might think. Everything I write is intended to alert my readers about what is going on in present time and bring to your attention the seriousness of the world around you. Countries don't just attack you without reason. These are not just random attacks on Americans. Something causes this type of action to happen. We install leaders in other countries to establish an alliance and strategic positioning. We attack other countries and then do our nation building to establish a presence and impose a democracy there, and we use the taxpayers' money to accomplish all of this. Our government works both ends against the middle, and it is a strategy that is catching up to these perpetrators. It has worked for a long time in theory to keep America a free country, but you must realize we wouldn't have enemies unless we created them, yet we remain attractive to the rest of the world because of our open and inviting presence in the world. We do have a lot to offer especially for those whom have been living under a dictatorship or under communism. And that is why we must continue to protect America at all cost.

This is America – a country for those who want and appreciate freedom of speech, freedom of religion, freedom of the press, free enterprise. This country is free and will remain free as long as we have people that will fight for their freedoms and protect their country and their rights to the bloody end. That includes confrontation within our ranks at times. However, we always get a few boobs infiltrating our government with their loose knitted mentality, always standing in the middle of the road trying to dictate to everyone their assessment of a twisted reality that wouldn't even get them out of the traffic on a slow day. And, because they have been enslaved by their own thoughts and government for so long and believe that having nothing is actually living, being told when to do whatever and how long to do it, is living the good life, they influence a few boobs like themselves and somebody starts a movement because they haven't had an original creative thought in their lives since they once contemplated suicide but didn't have the spine to even pull that off. That shows me what we really have in leadership is nothing more than a result of inbreeding. The American people, as I have stated numerous times, have had it with this kind of garbage in our government. This is going to end. The facts are in front of those whom we have given the authority to make decisions for the majority and to enact laws that are beneficial to all. If our government can't, or won't, fulfill the people's wishes, and especially again, with the facts in front of them, then it's time for them to go. We will get someone in there who has not been blinded with a common disease among politicians known as shit for brains. A little crude, but you get the point.

As you will see throughout this book, I will make specific points regarding issues I feel affect all of us. For that is the purpose after all, and from time to time I will revisit parts of this book that we have already been through, understanding that on the average, a person only retains a portion of what he or she reads. Therefore, by returning to points previously made as kind of an afterthought, we will have a more rewarding breakthrough to a clearer reality. Let's return to the tax issue for just a moment. Now just to get a different look at what tax is and how crooked it has become, go to www.freedomtofascism.com. You will get a good look at what Aaron Russo, the filmmaker, discovered while interviewing and documenting conversations regarding taxation. Now let's discuss what author and businessman Steve Forbes has to say regarding taxation.

According to Steve Forbes, we must repeal the 16th amendment before implementing the flat tax system. This would stop those cyclopic greed mongers and those thieving control freaks from imposing further taxation. Below is a list of countries that have already imposed the flat tax system and are having, as predicted, brilliant results with it. Their economies have leapt forward with tremendous growth and positive results. Governments have grown in more tax collection to the point that they are considering even more tax reduction to spur the economy on to a more positive and productive outcome.

Hong Kong, Romania, Slovakia, Russia, the Channel Islands of the Jersey and Guernsey including Lithuania are a few of the countries that are having tremendous success with a flat tax system.

Also looking to impose a flat tax are China, Spain, Croatia and other countries. America's state and treasury departments have become oblivious to these facts on purpose; not because they don't understand, but because they are trying to destroy the middle class. They are accustomed to an old and wrong way that keeps America behind as a leader and innovator in a new and positive world of discovery when we are capable and deserve to be in front of the curve with new and positive trends. Why else would we as a country be in debt to a foreign nation, i.e. China? In only three years after imposing a flat tax in Russia, Russia's tax collection more than doubled. So, don't tell me that a flat tax system doesn't work. Russia, as well as all the other countries that I just mentioned, has had an overwhelming success with the flat tax system. Wake up government! Wake up Washington! Wake up! Wake up! Whenever taxation is counter-productive and/or illegal, like what we have in America, the people will find a way around being robbed, and will find a way to create an underground or shadow economy, or as a last result, move their companies out of and away from an unfair system. That's only natural, but it's what's happening as a direct result of government gone deaf, dumb and blind to their own reality. With a flat tax system, the crooks as well as the corporations, who last year avoided over $18 billion in taxes as I mentioned earlier, would not escape paying their fair share of taxation. But this dumb ass government of ours wants to tax those who work hard and become successful. This dumb ass government wants to kill the people's incentive to become successful. This dumb ass government is a dumb ass government and every dumb ass that won't fight to correct their dumb ass government is a dumb ass indeed. Everybody under the flat tax system is treated the same. What is wrong with that Washington? What is your answer to the problems that you bureaucrats keep compounding! What do you find so attractive other than controlling, or stealing this society's money? Don't tell Americans that you're working on the problem. You've had years to fix the problem. If the rest of America dragged their asses like you people in Washington do, we would still be living in fucking caves! We the people are your employer and we have had all we're going to take from you. Do you get the picture? Other than communicating the dissatisfaction that the public has with the way that the government operates, and its seemingly lack of concern over numerous issues, I have to keep reminding myself that these are the same people that stood by and did nothing to save the life of Terri Schiavo. You remember the case of the woman named Terri Schiavo; the comatose lady that got so much press over the right of her husband to remove her from life support. Neither the Supreme Court nor then President George Bush would intervene. Judge Greer of Pinellas County, Florida gave the order to let her starve to death - murder her is more like it. So, I'm not surprised by the inaction of the Supreme Court and the judicial system regarding her case. They not only failed her miserably, they failed the entire community. They failed the entire American community. If they were going to kill her anyway, don't you think they could have been a little more humane by giving her a lethal injection instead of murdering that helpless woman by starving her to death? The headlines read "Terri Schiavo dies calm, peaceful, and gentle". That's crap!! When you are starved to death you do not die a peaceful calm and gentle death, your body screams for mercy and cramps from the abuse imposed on it, it is anything but gentle!! The absurd thing is that they believe we are stupid enough to believe that garbage. Look, there have been numerous cases of people who have for some unknown reason simply awakened from their coma after years. What was the reason for the rush to get this woman out of the way, too expensive to keep her alive? We can waste billions on illegal wars, but we can't give helpless people a chance? I ask you never to forget these injustices because that's what they want and expect you to do. This was cold-blooded murder, approved by Judge Greer of Pinellas County, Florida. Never forget it! And every chance you have to make that scumbag's life miserable, DO IT!! Do like he did to Terri

Schiavo, show no mercy, and don't ever stop!! We have nothing more than a cruel circus in some parts of our judicial, legislative and executive branches at times, but this performance of cruelty imposed on the innocent and helpless was one of absolute barbarism, similar to the practices of abortion performed by those who place no value on the human life! This disgusting insanity whirling out of control has permeated our society with such intoxicating addiction it is mind boggling at times. There is so much scandal in our government presently it's like the monkey is now loose and running the circus. Congress and the Senate are having a change of heart regarding the war in Iraq. Large oil companies are still raking in huge profits at the gas pumps, and we the American people are still paying outrageous prices. The American borders are overrun by illegal aliens flooding the United States. The oil for food scandal involves numerous foreign and domestic companies in the amount of billions of dollars, top aides giving up the identity of undercover agents; but I guess that's what happens when you have an administration that has no understanding of its own leadership. Even though former President "the decider" Bush, had to know there was no respect for his authority simply because his type of authority was out of step with America's reality. Still he had the audacity to want the control of America and without approval of the congress in an illegal war. He did more to damage the reputation of America during his election than we will be able to repair in a hundred years. He must have thought he could do anything that he wanted with your lives, your money, your future, and get away with it without responsibility attached. It seems this personality type always thinks chances are they won't get caught. The hell with honesty and integrity, just get what you can while you can get it and hope you don't get caught. But if you do get caught, just act stupid. Not hard for him, duh. That should be no problem, just claim you have no knowledge of any wrong-doing. You were just acting on information supplied to you by your own stupid administration. That seems to be the consensus everyone understands. You know from past experience for the most part that the fines the political law breakers will suffer won't even come close to the amounts they are able to steal and get away with.

I'll tell you what's getting ready to happen; you're getting ready to see the people take the power away from the politicians and impose a direct democracy with no wiggle room for anybody to ever take the power away from the American people ever again, period! And that means a total wipeout of the entire bunch. That means taking back control of the monetary systems, however, this maneuver, must not, cannot, by any means, ever land in the control of the Congress. The monetary system must be privatized. Not like the Federal Reserve though. That would mean that we could not just print money whenever we feel like it. That would mean that we would have a very serious responsibility attached and would demand that we as a country return to the gold standard. And because we have been off the gold standard for years, it only tells me that the Federal Reserve has been counterfeiting America's currency. Am I right Federal Reserve - printing worthless money? As it is now, the people of this country do not even know for sure the location of America's gold. Some say, Fort Knox, some say in the control of the Federal Reserve. For safe keeping…uummm….

Government has missed the point drastically and for some time, might I add. And on purpose, might I also add. Government is to serve the public's greater good, not self. And in doing so would benefit more than in their current state of thievery. But, they are so used to spending and wasting your money, they naturally must assume they have the right to it. It is we whom have allowed them such a mindset. When they eventually wake, they will find they have lost all power and have no future and absolutely no authority. There is a crime wave sweeping our government, and I'm very close to saying that I think almost everyone is a conspirator. Campaign promises are rarely ever kept. When asked direct questions we never get straight answers. The Supreme Court going off the deep end, using eminent domain laws to actually force a private citizen off of their land, and to give that illegally confiscated property to another private party as long as it produces a larger or broader tax base or fits into the scheme of serving the greater good. Are you kidding? That's absurd! That's insanity! That's communistic! But what do you expect from stupidity? Those people are so far off the track it's laughable, and still they have the audacity to call themselves Supreme Court justices. Actually, today's Supreme Court justices, in my opinion, are only three short of the dirty dozen!

Democrats are all over the Republicans accusing them of fraud, waste and abuse, and both the Republicans and Democrats are all over the federal government for failing to respond in a timely manner to disasters or secure our borders. The United Nations are in it up to their eyeballs, the director of FEMA has been fired but remains on the payroll at $165,000 salary per year. The Democrats invoke rule 21, the war in Iraq rages on, and indictments are flying around the White House like we've been attacked by the cast of "One Flew Over The Cuckoo's Nest". Is this what you bargained for in leadership? Is this what you're so proud of? Is this what you're so reverent of in your politicians? This is the biggest scam of our political history. There is so much hot air and natural gas on Capitol Hill, we as a nation should never have an energy shortage. ACORN alone has scammed this dumb ass government out of hundreds of millions of dollars. Our government can't control even the basic business of the day. Listen, back in the seventies there was a house of prostitution near Reno, Nevada, and I believe it was called the Mustang Ranch. The Mustang Ranch somehow got in trouble with the government, and the government took over the business of running the ranch. Well, a couple of years later the government went broke and had to close the ranch down. Now this is the funny part. The government says they are going to develop a government-run health care system for all of us idiots that can't figure it out for ourselves ok? Wait a minute, wait just one minute. You're selling sex and booze in a whore house, and you go broke? You have a government running a house of prostitution whereby the line of customers never stops, the business operates 24/7 you sell the cheapest booze, $5.00 cost per bottle and the inflated sale price per bottle is $200. The women do all the work and the government goes broke?

Don't forget that you, the taxpayer are paying for every stinking dime of this health care plan. What is wrong with this picture? You and I clearly and certainly must understand that government is not the answer to our health care problems and/or our needs. Government is not the answer to a society that knows more than the government will ever know. Government cannot respond to America's needs because it doesn't know how. Our government is purposefully deceptive. Our government is lying. Our government has no morals. Our own President is the enemy of this country. There have been 2.7 million jobs lost with the BO's stimulus package of $787 billion. France is a prime example of government not responding to the people's needs. The date is November 5, 2006 - "France - riots in the streets!"

My personal opinion is that this is only the beginning of retaliation toward oppressive governments that only take and rarely ever return values and opportunities to the people. You're going to hear your governments and politicians say this is no way to resolve the issues that are the social problems of the day. You're going to hear those same voices state that people need to use a lawful process to accomplish their goals to address any grievances. But that only makes sense to the guilty. That only makes sense to the powers that be. Because when they are out of touch with the people, they are also out of touch with all reality. As I stated earlier, this is exactly what needs to happen to get the attention of oppressive governments who only take and never give. This is what is going to continue to take place when the people are fed up with politicians and governments that are only interested in power and profit. Governments must ultimately remember this - the people are your power. Those pesky people are your success. The people are the engine that drives progress. Governments must wake to realize that they hold their position only because the people allow them the privilege and the people will remove them when they fail to respond with equality and opportunity for all. Unless the people responded to abuse and inequality with force and determination, other Mussolini's and Hitler's and Hussein's will emerge; including the Bush and BO types. History has proven that all power is corruptible and when our leadership and elected officials gain too much of that power, they are consumed and seem in most cases to develop tendencies less than human! ALWAYS!!!

There will always be problems with social issues, and yet we have some of the most wasteful stupid buffoons in charge of making progressive deals intended to eliminate and rectify these problems. We have one and a half billion dollars handed over to the people, strangers, who have said they will help us with some of the problems we have on the ground in Iraq, and the money just disappears. It was delivered and protected by three Blackhawk helicopters - delivered in cash! In cash! What baboon would fail to deliver the money to the rightful authorities and in increments as the work progresses? And, when the job finally finished and approved, the final payment be made. What idiot delivers cash paid upfront in a foreign country to the tune of $1.5 billion dollars, especially during a time of war? That's who we have running our country. God help us all.

Let's go to the United Nations for a moment. I believe that we have a maggot infestation in the United Nations from the bottom to the top, arrogant full of self. Pathetic cannot describe the pus gut maggots that have robbed the needy. The United States has been the largest contributor to the UN ever since it was first conceived. Angry cannot describe the way I feel or the way that you should feel over this absolute waste of an institution of this magnitude. While people are starving to death and having to live like animals just to survive, and at times watch their children die of malnutrition in their arms, you have these disciples of death stealing the very bread out of those children's mouths. Now, I am neither conservative or liberal, I'm a realist and a logical thinker. I am not politically correct, nor do I ever plan to be. I can understand crime out of desperation to survive. I can understand stealing to eat. I can understand self preservation. But I cannot ever understand looking at a starving child living one meal to the next, anguishing with every day that arrives, and taking even that away from them out of greed. These are the disciples of death and deserve to be imprisoned until they are forgotten like they have forgotten what it means to have compassion for their fellow human being. What a pitiful existence they must live. No human being can be that disconnected, and you as well as anyone else mean absolutely nothing to them. If you do not agree with their agenda, their plan, or their belief system, you are an enemy! When I hear the name Kofi Annan, I want to vomit. What a disgrace this man is. It hurts to call him a man. However, his memory will live in the hearts and minds of the ones he disadvantaged for decades. Knowing people like him is a lesson we should never forget. We just have to watch the company we keep so this kind of garbage never reoccurs. Kofi Annan was and has been a very painful and expensive lesson for the United States and the world. Not only monetarily speaking, but to thousands of disadvantaged souls who were robbed of what was rightfully theirs - a warm meal, clothes for their children, medical supplies for the sick. But he will live in luxury on the backs of all that missed out and all that he robbed. And you will continue to pay through forced government programs to support this kind of human dung. Disagree or not, you have no choice. Think it's not serious? It's serious alright. Forced government tax programs steal your money and spend it on this kind of shit and other garbage of which you are not even aware. What have the American people been doing with their authority? Why have we failed to use what is within our power to control? What is happening to our government? American Idol is exciting, while government, or the lack thereof, on the other hand is dull and boring. How wrong you are my misinformed prisoner of propaganda. If you will open some pages and start to educate yourself with any of the books I have mentioned, or that I will mention near the end of this book, I will guarantee you that you will catch a glimpse of a reality that you have never before seen. You may choose not to follow what could be a fantastic awakening; that is your choice, and I understand what you might see when you look at what we have in charge. But what is in charge should be everyone's focus and serious concern. But then, that may or may not be possible, depending on your will to fight for the better form of government. Fight these sleazy diseased maggots with what they don't understand. Fight them with awareness of the facts. They don't expect you to have any knowledge or perception of how government is run or should be run. They have attempted hiding the jewels and breaking the teeth of the constitution and the bill of rights that authorize you the control of government. Think of the awesome power you possess, and then realize this. Some, no most Americans don't know how to use such awesome controlling and authoritative power. That should shock you out of your complacency. You don't even know how to use the power and authority you have to control this country's destiny. Wake up now my seduced sleeping dreamers. The world has changed since you last looked. This is most important. There is something just beyond your reach that is more powerful than all the money you could count in a life time. Maybe you were meant to carry the torch for the whole of humanity. Have you ever thought of your own importance, or of your own responsibility in the realm of your present reality? Or is it that accepting the responsibility to get involved with what governs this country is just a little out of focus right now? Where would you start even if you could make a difference? Maybe when you see the major corporations of the world rip everybody off at the gas pumps would be a good start. We know our regulators are conveniently looking the other way while the corruption is taking place. Doesn't that make you want to kick somebody's ass? Our government continues to deceive us, use us, and sell us out for their benefit. Oil companies realize they can enslave us because our government officials are so indebted to them via lobbyists' influence, and have taken such large contributions from them, that they now must sell you out. Otherwise it just wouldn't be ethical not to honor the lobbyists whom have contributed so much to their campaigns. What's wrong with a little change of heart along the way? It's called serving two masters - that's what is wrong with it! It is also theft by deception!

The government that is paid to represent America's interests has given, and is continuing to give America's treasures away out the back door. And they know that you will do nothing about it! They refer to it as fair trade. Well, let's see if it is fair, then you make up your mind just how fair it really is. When you see Chrysler and General Motors closing plants in America because they can't compete with foreign auto makers, you have to do some investigating.

When America pays more tariffs to get cars into the foreign markets than foreign markets pay to get its automobiles into America, that's fair trade. When the same thing happens to Korean automobiles and now China soon to come aboard you are compelled to say 'who are you representing here'? That is fair trade.

You are getting your salary from the American taxpayer and you are representing everyone but the people who are paying you. That is fair trade, and you are a thief! You are a snake! You have sold your people out, and you will be dealt with. Thousands of people will lose their jobs and most likely their retirement. Possibly they will lose their homes, cars, and most certainly faith in their government. These are some of the snakes that now inhabit

America's government. These are the snakes that are in charge of keeping America financially stable by at least attempting to negotiate in the best interest of the American people and American businesses. Congress has shown what limp minded losers they are when they brought the recent oil executives in for questioning and failed to put them under oath. Handing them free rein to say and do as they please, and then not holding them responsible for the outright robbery of the American consumer. The measly little fines were nothing more than a joke. When major oil companies escaped prosecution and were allowed to abscond with billions of dollars ripped off from the American consumer in time of crisis, is nothing short of criminal, and I wouldn't be at all surprised when possibly some disgruntled autoworker whose life you let slip down the drain comes looking for you with a baseball bat in his hand. This government, whose job it is to protect America's interests, is about as much in charge of leading as the garbage that I threw out yesterday.

Our government is negotiating away from America's interests. I say our government, actually, our government now belongs to the lobbyists and radical agencies like the World Trade Organization, who now tell America what we must do to satisfy their agenda by bringing regulation in line with international law. Even though we pay our congressmen in excess of $165,000 dollars annual salary each, including all they can steal through illegal trips, gifts, vacations, outings, hotels and hookers, and sometimes a few hours work, if you can call a bridge to nowhere work. Lobbyists and foreign government agencies are the ones that seem to have our government's full attention. Even though, President BO promises change, it appears that it's a change for the worse. You can bet that our dear congressmen that walk away from these lobbyists controlled congressional gatherings, also walk away with the biggest change, in their pockets. There are only a few senators and congressmen that I would trust to take control of my garbage. And even those are blocked by the majority of the termites that are eating away at America's now fragile foundation. I am appealing to you to join together and push through the political impaction that keeps you and me and the majority of the American people from enjoying even the basic freedoms that the founding fathers intended and guaranteed all of us; our children, our grandchildren, and America's future generations.

It isn't enough to outsource American jobs to foreign countries. The government that is in control of running this country wants to bring other governments to America to run this country's ports. Do you remember what I said earlier, that when the dog catches the scent of food, nothing will keep it from getting its nose under the tent, and that it will eventually find a way inside? Well, truer words have never been spoken when you take a closer look at what is happening to American business in this country. This government of the American people is slowly giving away America's interests, its security, its jobs, its treasures. Look at the American government and how it is slowly being taken over by the termite/czars on every level, and no one is doing anything about it. The owners of this country are the American people, and they are allowing our trusted government to bring in any and everyone to live as they wish, to take what they want. In fact, we pay them to keep it, to deface and never repair it, to own it, to buy and sell it as they please, when the rightful heirs to the treasures and the property who have worked and died to protect it are shut out in the cold! We are told to be tolerant of others. Be generous to those less fortunate than yourself. Just open your doors and let anyone who wants to move in do so. Allow anyone and everyone to just help themselves, they mean you no harm. So what that the majority of the alleged terrorists that destroyed the trade towers came from the same country. Try them in civil courts. So what that the same group is now taking control of your shipping ports, no big deal. Don't be suspicious. The next move will be to bring in some biological weapons or undetected nuclear weaponry. The termites that you let inhabit your house have now eaten away at its foundation to the point that it collapses from within and all you have left is a pile of rubble that once was a shining example of the greatest nation on earth. But like history has proven and continues to prove, great and majestic empires have collapsed and faded into the past only to become content in the history books. Nothing will last forever, so accept the inevitable. That is the ultimate form of progress; somewhere in the distant future other generations will make the exciting discovery that this was America. Yes, this was once the United States. This was the greatest nation in all the world until the people lost their grasp and simply surrendered control to their government's own creative corruption campaigns brought on by those in charge of protecting at all cost, the interests of the country and the safety of the American people. Corrupt does not begin to explain the Obama administration and the absolute devastation that awaits the American people if they continue to follow this pied piper of insanity. To put your faith in what is being presented through our present government is insanity and will surely shut the American people out of their rightful ownership of this country. Don't be fooled into thinking you have no control.

My friends, we are on the brink of a major unnatural disaster and worse, an unnecessary one. Governments that refuse to be responsible and accountable to the citizens do not deserve the right of leadership and the tax revenue from those same citizens. Those citizens therefore in my opinion have the right to respond accordingly to the robbery of their belongings. Meaning forced programs, meaning extortion. And that is all it is without proper representation. Citizens that have such leadership, have a responsibility to each other as citizens, to join forces and fight for their legal constitutional rights, and defeat, by whatever means, THESE OUTLAW GOVERNMENTS. Using whatever means to wage warfare against such tyranny and illegal possession of power. When a government refuses to listen to the people, it needs to be overthrown! However, today's people have become so confused and are so accustomed to being robbed, that no one thinks much about it, or is it that anyone can or will do anything about it. So on it goes, same shit different day. How many times have you heard today's government officials say, "I will take full responsibility for what has happened as a result of a ... blah, blah, blah". But that's just more garbage mouth from the ass of intelligence that runs this country. It's just lip service that makes the person stating that bull shit appear to seem responsible. If jail time, penalties and fines were considered along with the admitted responsibility of this verbal bravery it's likely none of these types would be able to utter a word. They would all of a sudden be struck deaf, dumb and blind and unable to utter a sound - OTHER THAN THE ONE COMING FROM THE SEAT OF THEIR PANTS. So just read into that crap what it really is. This is not failure of a government who is trying. This is intentional and criminal. It's beyond shallow to blame the establishment and not the people who run it. But that is the mindset of the ones in charge. Just scrap the institution and start over! Oh, really? And you want who to pay for it this time? And where do you arrive at the authority to dismiss the people who pay for it all? Sometimes, actually most of the time, when governments become overconfident and have too much power over the citizens, they seem to go on some sort of self destructive auto pilot. Oh yeah, just put it on auto pilot, it will take years before anyone catches on. And in the meantime we catch a few rounds of golf, go on a few cruises with some hookers at the expense of the taxpayer, charge some jewelry on our slimy little government paid expense card and just enjoy the perks while we can. No one will ever be the wiser. When this kind of mindset is our leadership's priority you must be aware that we are way off course and in dangerous waters. This is perfect timing for those watching and waiting to send the fatal blow to the unsuspecting. Sad as it may sound and sad as it may be, I am beginning to see the ugly head of dictatorship being born in the United States. And though we are not always privileged to all of the inner workings of our government, which is very evident, sometimes we do get a glimpse at the information and facts they try to hide from us. If you really put things together about what is happening and who is protecting Americans from more so called terrorist attacks, you will not sleep very peacefully at night. Stop here and go to www.zeitgeist.com. Again and Click on the photo that depicts the three wise men at the manger on the upper left of the screen and watch the section where the planes are crashing into the World Trade Center. There are three sections to this web viewing and you may watch all if you are interested, but I want you to watch with absolute attention the ones that I just mentioned. Can we as Americans really ever trust our own government with national security? Do you realize that even after the terrorists supposedly hit the World Trade towers and died in the process, those terrorists who were training to be pilots, received their pilot's license in the mail weeks later? Which raises the question, why would you train a pilot who told you that they didn't want to learn how to fly a plane whereby you had to learn to take off and land? Doesn't that raise a red flag in someone's mind? Not if it's planned! Well, that makes about as much sense as wanting those from the Arab countries to run our ports, right Bush? But our former president didn't mind. He also doesn't mind that the majority of illegal aliens entering this country come across our borders from Mexico. And the majority of those aren't Mexican-nationals looking for work. This is America, and America needs to be run by Americans. It doesn't matter what nationality you are as long as you are a legal American citizen. Try crossing into Korea, China or Russia without permission or an invitation from that government, and you will be arrested and accused of spying. You will be sentenced most likely to years of hard labor and unimaginable abuses, deprived of any rights and forgotten, period! UNLESS BOUNCING LITTLE BILL CLINTON COMES TO RESCUE YOU. And he certainly will if there are women involved and you have a live television camera running. We on the other hand are a mixing pot of races, but we have gone through the process of becoming legalized citizens, or we are natural born citizens of this country. The statue of liberty is our symbol of freedom, and we will bend over backwards to help other countries or people who are willing to become citizens of the United States. But we will stand our ground against those who would disrespect our country and threaten our freedoms. And that means just that. Although I believe we have people working in our government who are our enemy and would sell us down the river for a laugh. I believe that we have people living in this country who plan to destroy us from the inside with whatever means possible. I believe that we have people in our military that plan to destroy us from the inside, as proven in the Fort Hood massacre of our own troops. This is the proof about which I speak throughout this book. We are so politically correct that we don't even stop people who obviously operate out in the open, as was in the Fort Hood case. Here was a Major in the military who stated his Muslim allegiance openly and was detected many times acknowledging a Muslim ideology that had all the earmarks of what could be explosive at any time, and we just go on about our business like it was just another day. I blame this Major's superior officers for the dead and wounded of Fort Hood's fallen. We pay more attention to political correctness than to those who would infiltrate our troops. But why should that bother us, we have a Muslim as a president. I believe we have a president that is going to do his best to destroy America as quickly as he can because, suddenly people are onto him and they are following the scent of America's intended destruction. America is also beginning to see what has been hidden for a long time, but now is coming into plain view. We need to look closer at whom we have in charge and who would waste our resources and break us financially by gaining control of strategic powers in our government. For too long we have given away Americas treasures to foreign entities, but when I heard former president George W. Bush say he would veto any bill that comes to him regarding stopping our ports from being run by Arabs, I began to have second thoughts about which side he is really on. If there is a side anymore! I understand sending signals by your actions, and I understand what has really happened here, our government has been sending the wrong signals for a long time to those who would harm us. When attacks against Americans came against foreign military establishments and Americans died, our government did nothing - wrong signal. When airplanes were shot down in international air space with Americans aboard, and all died, our government did nothing - wrong signal. When the USS Cole was attacked, and military personnel died, our government did nothing -

wrong signal. And now that untold millions of illegal aliens are in this country, our government is continuing to do nothing again, but pick up the tab for them at the taxpayer's expense - wrong signal again! Our government is more concerned about what the rest of the world's opinion is of them than what we Americans know of them. We recognize the tree by the fruit it bears, which is something our government obviously doesn't understand, and obviously isn't concerned with. So let me remind them that they are sending the wrong signal to the American people once again and that should be above all their major concern! As of February 25, 2006, President Bush offered to rebuild the shrine that was destroyed in the Iraqi conflict. Hold it! Hold it! Hold it! You are not finished with Katrina yet. You are not finished rebuilding the tragedies in America yet. Is this where our government's priorities lie? You want to start to rebuild shrines in the Middle East? I hope you're paying for it out of your pocket this time big boy, because we are sick of it. And we're sick of you, and sick of those like you. Those people don't want your grubby little fingers in their religion anyway. They hate you. You are an infidel in their eyes. What is wrong with this government? We're sick of every administration making promises to Americans that they never intend on keeping, but yet are willing to bend over backwards for foreign nations at our people's expense. And I'm speaking for every person in America who demands that this government be responsible to America first. We are the people who are telling you how stupid you are and what idiots you look like to the rest of the world. We will replace you with people who have a brain, one that functions in the realm of this present reality, not those that only know how to authorize and afford you the power to communicate your fucking generosity to the rest of the world at our expense - get it? Why in the name of hell would you want to rebuild a destroyed shrine that does not concern you? This kind of tragic unrest has been going on for years in that region, and it's an insult to those people for you to put your hands on their religious problems. They are rich with oil and other natural resources and can afford to rebuild their shrines in the way that they have done for years. You obviously think that money is the answer to everything. It is not! Those people are not Chrysler. They are not the same as some financial institution that you will invest in and control like you are attempting here in the United States.

And while we're on the subject of blatant stupidity, the American people need to push to dismantle, abolish, eliminate and destroy the Electoral College which ultimately decides by vote, who will be President of the United States. We will have none of that shit any longer. No wonder we have no voice in our government; we have turned over all of our power to the agency who at one time convinced the American people that they needed to put their trust and confidence in a representative known as a politician who would vote for you, because maybe you could not get to town that easily, and you were needed on the farm to take care of Granny's goat. Well Granny's goat died anyway, and the countryside is now the city and we have become a little more sophisticated and a little smarter about blood sucking politicians and the many faces they wear. In all reality, listen to me now, we have never voted as long as we have allowed the electorate to act on our behalf, we only wasted our time and energy. And that's why in all reality no one in Washington gives a damn about what we think or how we vote because we don't even have enough sense about ourselves to maintain our own independent responsibility. Could be that this is why we have Communist Chinese running our seaports in Long Beach, California and Arab's taking over seaports with the blessing of our politicians. They are calling it a security leak that the American people even found out that this was happening to our ports. Well, is this what we want - foreigners running our government? Is having an abusive and illegal agency that steals your money through forced taxation something we the American people want? Is having runaway debt something we the American people want? Is having a wasteful government something the American people want? Do you want secret agencies making decisions that doesn't require them to alert their superiors of their actions or decisions prior to entering your home, your bank account, or accessing your medical records without your knowledge, wiretapping your phone calls and e-mails? Well that is what is happening and I have to ask you once again, is that what you want? You need to learn the meaning of the word, de facto... which means step aside stupid taxpaying citizen, you have no authority here. We know what's best for you and the rest of society. If we want anything from you we'll call on you around tax time. De facto means, a one party system; this is our decision and our choice; you have no say in this. So you see, it really doesn't make any difference which party wins, you lose! It isn't enough to find out that the Arabs want to run our ports, but now we find that they want control of our strategic missile and manufacturing components as well. Keep your eye on your congressman and your lobbyists and international decision makers. They're all devolving into one stinking cesspool. Time to wake up America! Does it look like someone is trying to slip another one in on America by strategic positioning? Call me suspicious, call me an alarmist, I'm screaming foul as loud as I can. Warning! Warning! Warning! This is not some, Chicken Little propaganda, running through the neighborhood screaming "the sky is falling, the sky is falling." We are the ones with our eyes open. We are allowing our democracy, our country, to be torn to pieces and divided among these parasitic wolves! Can you blame the American public for accusing the government of no transparency? They do their secret little deals and then try to hide what they have done from the American people! Do you blame the American people for feeling disenfranchised? I really have a deep appreciation for this country and for those who made it great. I have a great admiration for those whose generosity and saving grace extends to the far reaches of the earth to retrieve some disfigured child who has suffered some horrifying accident or birth defect, correcting what might have otherwise been a wasted life for which no one else cared. I appreciate those politicians who scoff at lobbyists sucking at their toes like the parasites the rest of us can identify without having to be in their stinking presence. When you mention balanced-budget, our government turns a deaf ear, and when you realize that our currency is counterfeit, thanks to former president Nixon, who in 1971 permanently took America off the gold standard, you will realize you are on a sinking ship. Shut up taxpayer, we'll spend your money the way we see fit and we'll drive you so far into debt that it will take not only your lifetime to pay it off but your children's and their children's lifetimes as well! Do you realize that as of March 2006, the United States was faced with default on our national debt! But this Congress doesn't hear you because you have no representation in Washington! I dare you to get involved in reclaiming this country. I double dog dare you. It's your country anyway! Let's write a page in American history that sends a message to the ones that we elect in the future. Let's send a message so strong that the political opportunist would scatter like the cockroaches they are. A message that says when you work for the American people, you work for the greatest nation on earth. Let's write a page in history that lives up to America's reputation, a page that is reasonable and beneficial to all Americans whom have invested in this country by their sacrifice, their tax money and their commitment to bring about accountability of the elected officials regardless of the level they serve. It amazes me that we the American people have just let our government squander and waste and tax us into oblivion. I know that I'm making statements that are going to make some people uncomfortable. GOOD! And I know that sometimes I am repeating myself, but all this is necessary. I know that I'm hitting some nerves, but I know also that I am revealing the hard-core truth that smacks the low life political scum in the face! The truth we've all played a part in the destruction of this great house of the people that now is showing signs of collapsing from within. We, the American people, are guilty for not cleaning our house on a regular and timely plan. America, it's time to wake up and go to work on repairing this great house of the people, or we're going to cease living in a free society. We have work to do! And I mean today. Today is the day of reckoning. Today is the day we start by demanding responsibility from the free loaders that are destroying our government and our nation. Nothing happens by accident. Everything is intentional, and most Americans have no clue what has been going on right under their noses. They just wake, go to work, repeat the process until they are no more; never to have realized the freedom that was theirs, never to have realized the riches that was theirs, never to have realized that they were being robbed of their birthright. Ignorance is not bliss my friends.

In 2005, over 11,000 workers were laid off because their jobs were moved overseas, and over 16,000 jobs were outsourced and over 11 million illegal people were suspected of crossing into the United States. In my opinion, it's time to outsource some congressmen and some senators and others who have been deliberately sleeping on their watch and all the time getting paid with our tax money. Let's roust them out of their comatose state with an alarm so loud that their state of complacency is shattered with no tolerance for the official that has only self interest in mind. We have no use for the elected official who represents foreign interests while being paid by the American taxpayer. Reaching for their paycheck with one hand and stabbing you in the back with the other will not fly any longer.

Representative Duncan Hunter, Republican of California, plans to introduce a plan to kill the Dubai ports deal that was planned for March 6. It is in direct opposition of what former President Bush has proposed. Bush said he would veto any legislation that comes his way regarding the deal. Representative Duncan Hunter's bill would demand 100% inspection of all cargo coming into the United States. While some will argue that the Arabs have helped the U.S. in the past is not to be denied. We have helped them as well. We have made them rich by buying their oil, yes? The ports deal with Dubai is all about the idea of allowing a foreign entity to run our sea ports. That had to be conceived by a mentally deficient blob or group of blobs known as CIFUS (Committee on Foreign Investments in the United States).

Which should stand for, 'certified idiots found operating in the United States'.

As of March 2, 2006, and before, serious meetings were being held to do something about this out-of-control government. There is talk of impeachment of the President for his stiff arm tactics against the people of the United States, but we all know this is just saber rattling and according to John Conyers, ranking member of the judiciary committee, Democrat of Michigan, John Dean, and former member and adviser to President Nixon, Elizabeth Holtzman, Harper's Magazine, Lewis Lapman, editor of Harper's Magazine and others stated, that if this Congress and Senate don't do anything to get some answers and see some accountability from their current administration, then they would form pressure groups to get rid of this group of lame dorks this coming election. We as a society of citizens do not have to take this crap from the government! Now I don't think the American citizens realize how much power is in their hands, but once a groundswell of opposition goes against the bad administration, bad decisions, and the court of public opinion is strong and determined the government had better listen. That's the power that we the people have. Don't forget it!

These political warts have little time to get the job done or get the hell out of office if it's beyond their capacity to perform in a proper and meaningful capacity! If it weren't for the attitude where the elected official thinks that he or she is beyond reproach and not responsible to respond to the American people, we wouldn't be having this illegal alien problem at our borders today. We wouldn't have Congressman William Jefferson hiding $90,000 in cash in his freezer and denying any wrongdoing. The very same types that are, and always have been nonproductive in their capacity as appointed officials in the past, as well as the present, are the very problem America always faces. The American people have always had to go back and clean up the politicians' mess, bail out the overspending, correct the mistakes and then become responsible for more of a tax burden while correcting the mistakes made by the politicians that we keep electing. Are you sick of it yet? We listen to their speeches on one hand and applaud them for all their eloquent oratory and empty promises like they're going to keep any of them. Right, OBAMA? We waste our time listening to feel good messages and temporary hope gatherings knowing that it is all really just a waste of time and a bunch of crap. There is no long lasting hope in ever placing your trust in the human element, but that is all there is, so that tells me that we will have to be careful of what we elect. There is only hope in action and holding those whom you have entrusted accountable and nothing more. They make a contract with America, knowing it's just more empty words and promises; words as empty as all the promises made before. But it sounds good and like little kids sucking their thumbs, we remain in awe and fail to want to recognize the deception and most of all don't hold accountable those that lie to us at every opportunity - knowing all the time we will be disappointed and do nothing about it but complain later. We will even deny we voted for the lazy scumbags as we watch them cost Americans another war and more financial disruption. It never ends! It never gets any better, all the promises of tax cuts, no more wars, secure borders, peace, more jobs, less unemployment, lower gas prices, better health care, lower cost of living for the elderly. Where is it? Can you feel the bands of restraint getting tighter every time you ask about broken campaign promises or disagree with the status quo? Where are all the promises of a balanced budget, lower taxes, better and more jobs? Where is it any better? I see government taking over the failed financial institutions. I see government controlling auto makers and private enterprise and driving them out of business. I see stimulus packages in the multi-billions of dollars illegally taken from the taxpayer and given to private industry without allowing the taxpayer their constitutional right to vote on such matters. To deny the people that right is in fact a constitutional breach and is illegal. I see legal matters conveniently being overlooked. I also see SOCIALISM AND MARXISM.

If the people who write our laws won't enforce or abide by our laws, what good are they to the population who support them? Ooh, those laws must have been meant for everybody else. This is going to sound old and over used, but the government is employed by the American people who pay them their outrageous salaries for the work they do, or don't do, emphasis on the latter. If you have an employee who refuses to do the job you have assigned them, what do you do? Do you continue writing them a check every week?

Well that's what we do. If you have an employee who refuses to work or even show up to work every week, do you continue writing them a check every week? Well that's what we do. That's what congress does! We have allowed the government to rob us any and every time we put our trust in them. They have insulated themselves with laws that they write to the point that it takes an act of Congress to prosecute them for any wrongdoing or recall them for any of the same. We are not watching closely enough. My friends, we are the crazy ones for not coming together and putting the fear of God in these useless human hemorrhoids, whether Democrat, Republican, or Independent. Thomas Jefferson said, "When the people fear their government you have tyranny, when the government fear the people, you have liberty". Our Government has embezzled America's trust. I guess they thought that the American people would never live long enough or become smart enough or realize they were being robbed of everything right down to their loose change. The same goes for the 9/11 trade tower destruction. Our government knew what was going to happen just like they knew what was going to happen at Pearl Harbor. A skilled combatant or opponent takes advantage of weak moments to gain the upper hand. This statement may be a little premature, and I may recant later on but let's begin to put the blame where it belongs and hold accountable those whom are guilty for thousands of innocent lives lost and great symbols of American prosperity wiped from the face of this earth. Sure the enemy will strike, but why? They have before - what's new? Now analyze the data and come up with some lame excuse to try to convince anyone with a brain cell that it was out of our control. A lot of conspiracy theorists think 9/11 was an inside job. Just like Pearl Harbor was an inside job. I want you to make up your minds after you have had the opportunity to view the facts. Please visit www.zeitgeist.com again, and watch it again. Remember to click on the thumbnail that depicts the manger scene with the three wise men and the Christ child. This is a website that has three parts to it. You have to watch it all the way through a couple of times. Then I want you to go to the website www.freedomtofascism.com again. That website is produced and hosted by film producer, Aaron Russo. After you have watched those videos, stop for a moment before jumping to conclusions and ponder the possibility of enemies of this nation living and working along side you in the workplace like those living and working in this country that supported Hitler during that war. Some of our elected officials have always had dirty hands. That's why we have a Federal Reserve System. That's why we have an IRS system specifically designed to rob you at will and keep you enslaved permanently. We need accountable reform in this country and it needs to start in Washington, D.C., and that would take about five minutes and a big stick. Pick up a copy of "Fleeced" by Dick Morris and Eileen McGann, published by Harper Books. We seem to forget that the law is the law and that all compassion for the lawbreakers goes out the window if breaking the law is intentional. I believe that if the law is broken on purpose with reckless disregard, then the law should be dispensed at full force. Not like in the Clinton impeachment case. Old, crooked-finger, Cigar Bill gave the finger to the American people and walked because he was an elected official. He was the President. In other words, a crime is not a crime if the President commits it? As in the case of President George W. Bush, murder would not be murder if he wrongly goes to war and thousands of innocent lives are lost. They were all just in the way I suppose, and the (barf), President was in a hurry, huh? He and Chaney are going to walk away from this bloodbath and destruction thinking that they got away with it. But while their cronies pat them on the back and call them great statesmen, we know they are no better than Hitler and his minions were.

You must realize there is always the possibility of a problem with the people whom we put in charge of running this great country. Now, since we are aware that we have to correct or monitor these problems because it seems the majority of the human race has a propensity to become destructive once given the exclusive power and authority to make such high level decisions, especially when it comes to dispensing and dictating such authority. This problem has always been around. This problem did not start with our society. This problem has existed and been handed down throughout history. Our laws say you can't come to this country illegally. Well, really? Millions of people have, and they are still here! There are people who have been in this United States for many years, illegally. Well that wasn't hard so maybe they can get the relatives in also. And on it goes. But we have anywhere from 12 to

25 million illegal aliens in America. What do you do to police that many illegal aliens in a society when we don't even know who or where they are? Would you say we should fast track them all to American citizenship and bypass all the American system requirements, and OOH YEA, also bypass the other people that have played by the rules and have been waiting for years at the chance of becoming an American citizen.

Well it's mid-November 2009, and that's just what Napolitano has done. Would you be willing to agree, that the quality of life in America is eroding? But wait! There's more. When government needs money, then government will change the rules of law to favor their agenda. They will do what they once would prosecute you for doing as long as Taxable income from selling marijuana or those 12 to 25 million illegal aliens whom are now fast tracked to legalized American citizenship, pay tax to the IRS. Thats money that once was sent to other countries, and the IRS was left only with attempts to prosecute legalized citizens for allegedly owing $1.16, as was the case of the Ohio woman. What a relief that must be huh? So you've taken the jobs away from those who are here legally and now jobs disappear from those who have a legal right to be here. The quality of life starts to diminish all around you. The carpet layers, the auto workers, the convenience store workers, the truckers, and the computer and technology workforce. Are you starting to get the picture? All the legal citizens deserve to be here and deserve the rights and freedoms because they have earned them. Use the following example: You work hard to live the lifestyle you choose. You buy a house, a car, and you work years to secure your future. Then one day you go to work and your boss tells you that you have been laid off due to an overabundance of workers in your field. Eventually you run out of options, you can't find a job, you can't afford to pay for the house or the car, and you can't afford to go to school either - so you are forced to sell your house and car and then shortly you're out of money. You don't have a job, or a place to live, and you see no future. All of this because your politicians did not do their jobs in protecting the borders, and there's nothing you can do about it. However, your politicians were paid handsomely to do nothing and as a result you get to become homeless! Well, if you don't want that to happen to you or yours, then you and the rest of America had better show this brand of politician the door with a swift kick in the ass, or one day in the not too distant future you will wake up to find everyone around you is of another race and speaks very little English. Everyone is afraid to speak out and organize because times have changed, and to do so would be a crime against the state. People have ended up missing and never heard of again just for speaking their minds. So everyone does nothing just like before, and that's what the government ultimately wants!

They want you to shut up! And they want people like me to shut up! And before they try and get their way, you and I and people like us had better get together and demand some changes because for right now we still have a voice and some backbone and some courage and some will. We still have clear vision, and we still have a fire in our bellies, and it is our kind of people that get things done for the rest of society. It is time to demand that this leadership secure our borders because if not, we will see a collapsed economy and a non-secure and chaotic society. Now listen closely, we are a society of immigrants, but legal immigrants, and we in America, have the welcome mat out for those who will come into this society as a legal citizen to be respectful of our laws and our culture. The very fact that I have the right to write this book is a perfect example. I'll stand behind this country 200% because I have that right. Not some legislative right to express my distaste with some of the people who are employed by this country, but by my God-given right, my human right. No man, woman, or law gave it to me, and no man woman or law will take it from me. That is the beautiful place that I live called America! You want to live here? Then get in line and learn to speak the language, obey the laws, and contribute to the society that affords you the freedoms and the opportunities for success. Coming here in any other way is fraudulent, and you are guilty of forcing yourself on a society that will not tolerate it. Many of the people in America know what it means to experience hardship, struggles, bad luck and failure, but we also know that tomorrow is another day. And tomorrow will be different because our society and the way we are structured allows for you and me to get up and have another go at it if we don't make it the first time. It will allow and offer you even more if you will conform to the way this country functions. If not, I feel sorry for you because you are missing an opportunity of a lifetime. You are missing an opportunity that you may never get again. So let's get back to the point. As I have stated before, you can't blame the underdog for trying to rise to the next level. You can't blame your opponent for wanting to win the fight for survival, contest, or lover, including war. But, we as Americans have a responsibility to our country and to each other. Now some people get voted into office and are given the responsibility and privilege to serve this country but they are fraudulent. They take the taxpayers money in a form of a paycheck and fail to deliver on their campaign promises. Instead they get caught up in the Washington machinery that robs America of its wealth by sending foreign countries America's jobs. I don't care how you look at it. It's those representatives who are traitors. It goes much deeper than that though, it goes back centuries, and to ancient times. Politicians are all the same. It doesn't make any difference when or where you find them. Take a dna sample from all of them and you'll find they are all from the same cesspool. They are all of one mind set. Take, take, take - conquer, possess, hoard, self indulge - destroy your own if necessary to maintain control. Even as in the case of Jesus himself. Need I say more? Therefore in today's case look no further than Washington, DC, and visualize if you will, laws being written every day to take more and more from you….a penny, a nickel, a dime at a time. You can count on one hand the presidents that were seemingly trustworthy. You have to think, what person would spend millions of dollars on campaigning to win a congressional seat or the presidency that only pays a few hundred thousand dollars each year. They wouldn't do it if it were their money. But it's not just money they're after, it's power. Its power and control over people's lives, power to dictate policies, power that makes history, good or bad. And in certain cases, the desire to be feared! They wouldn't do it if they didn't have a separate or personal agenda, a backroom deal whereby the connection is to something much larger. But they'll take from the lobbyists, and they will be committed to the lobbyists, and you can just wait! I blame politicians for hundreds of thousands of murders of the unborn, via abortion! And the absolute garbage we call the Supreme Court for giving way to Roe vs. Wade, the ruthless murderous women who promote and participate in the destruction of the innocent unborn. The passing of the law to legally allow the murder of innocent unborn children is insanity. If there is a just God, those sins could not be forgiven. Then you have Congresswoman McKinney, striking a Capitol police officer for detaining her when she tried to breach a security gate. He should have done his job and cuffed that thing and put her ugly ass in jail for striking a police officer. The same as the police do when a citizen touches a police officer during any confrontation. That's the process, if the politicians have the right to break the law or to strike an officer for doing his or her job, then think what the American people have waiting for these politicians who get paid to do their jobs but never do. Process that! Or when you base a war on faulty intelligence that caused thousands of deaths, you and your entire cabinet of mass murderers need to face the consequences! I don't care if you are a president or a dictator, communist or free. You just cannot engage in battle or abort the innocent or the helpless and say this is just collateral damage and walk away without consequences. You cannot just waste your country's resources without answering to the charges. You cannot just give away sovereign territories or land of the United States as you did with the Panama Canal. Where are the leaders and the leadership that we pay for? Where is the responsibility? I hear radio talk show hosts address this problem everyday, and I hear people responding to questions posed by the radio host with sometimes very qualified solutions. But I never hear or see anyone follow through with taking action and faith that what they want to happen will happen. It takes action, but just like many past incidents the government knows they can outlast you, and they also know that you will quit before you see your plan come to completion. The only thing government understands is fear and intensity. I recall the Watts California riots when the black community grew tired with what was happening in society, so they rioted and burned down the whole damned city. But they got the attention of the government, and things changed for the African-American community. I see the people demanding from the government that they find qualified solutions before engaging in unlawful and illegal wars and illegal unlawful taxation to pay for it all! Look, as long as you are alive, you will pay in some way for this country. That should tell you very clearly that you have a voice in this government. So demand the freedom and the authority to speak your mind - to condemn a government of its wrongdoing and wasteful practices is not unpatriotic. If you're like me, you're mostly tired of asking, after having already paid for the job to get done. I, expect those politicians that have been elected for a specific reason not to fail me as an American. Or if they do, as an investor in this country, explain to my satisfaction. TO MY SATISFACTION, what went wrong and why!!! When you tell me that you will take full responsibility if it happened on your watch, I want to see you keep your promise! LIP SERVICE IS OVER!! It is disgusting the way America is headed. And, it is disgusting that the politicians have let the American people down to this point.

Again I ask, where did the money that was in the Social Security fund go? It didn't just fall out of pocket. Where is Americas gold? It just didn't accidentally get misplaced, it was not an accidental cover up by the President to try and privatize Social Security, but to use the excuse that the Social Security is going broke because there aren't enough people paying into it is fraudulent! The naked truth is, there are more people taking out of the Social Security fund that have no business taking the money out in the first place, and I mean un-authorized people, i.e. politicians, authorizing aliens undeserved set amounts of Social Security funds that never have to be paid back. Paying people out of the fund that have never contributed to the fund. Taking money out for other programs that hopefully will make these generosity thieves look good in someone else's eyes. People that work in our government are leaving empty IOU's, and never honoring those IOU's. They have no intention of ever repaying what they have literally stolen from the American people. In this as well as any other business, that is called misappropriation of funds, or fraud, and that caries with it a lawful and legal penalty because it is deceptive and fraudulent! Just not in Washington I suppose. What gets me is you don't see anybody responding in outrage and demanding from government the names of the ones responsible for taking the people's money, or giving it to those who don't deserve or have legitimate right to it. They are embezzling the people's money! Embezzlement means to steal - like in Enron, in robbery - like in IRS, like in what people go to jail for every day in the real world. We hear politicians lying to the American people every day. We know they are robbing us blind, failing to do their jobs, walking away from the responsibility they accepted when they were elected! I hear people responding with, what do you expect from politicians? To expect anything different would be delusional. Side stepping the questions and responding with empty rhetoric and convoluted answers leads me to believe that they don't even know what they've said. The following is an e-mail that I received in 2008. I don't know who the author of this information is. It was one of those, pass this on type of emails, but it sure nails it for me. "IF AN IMMIGRANT IS OVER THE AGE OF 65, THEY CAN APPLY FOR SOCIAL SECURITY AND GET MORE THAN A WORKER THAT WORKED AND CONTRIBUTED TO THE FUND FROM 1944 TO 2004. IT IS INTERESTING THAT THE FEDERAL GOVERNMENT PROVIDES A SINGLE REFUGEE WITH A MONTHLY ALLOWANCE OF $1,890.00, AND EACH CAN OBTAIN AN ADDITIONAL $580.00 IN SOCIAL SECURITY ASSISTANCE FOR A TOTAL OF $2,470.00 PER MONTH, AND THEY NEVER HAVE TO REPAY ANY OF THAT MONEY. NOT EVEN THE SOCIAL SECURITY MONEY THAT OUR GOVERNMENT SO EAGERLY AND GENEROUSLY GIVES AWAY TO THOSE THAT NEVER CONTRIBUTED." That my friend is socialism, communism, Marxism. And that's why the Social Security system is going broke. NOT BECAUSE THERE AREN'T ENOUGH PEOPLE CONTRIBUTING TO THE SOCIAL SECURITY FUND! NOW THAT YOU KNOW THIS, WHERE IS THE OUTRAGE? WHERE IS THE REVOLUTION?

California State Senator Romero is now stating that she represents both illegal and legalized citizens. This is a State Senator that has just told you that even though you pay her salary, she is going to represent the very ones that threatened your way of life and your freedoms, and possibly your existence. If there are levels of stupidity, then she has just scored the highest you can score. This idiot just scored the highest you can score with me. She has just shoved our constitutional rights up our noses, and that in part is the very reason I'm writing this book. This woman is a traitor to the American people. If we American's are represented this way by our elected officials and do not send this woman packing, then there is something very wrong with us. We as Americans talk about freedom, and at face value that looks and sounds good but the price for freedom must be paid by someone. And it comes at great sacrifice most of the time. Have we forgotten the people that continue to give their all, and too much of the time pay the ultimate to keep this nation safe and free? To not respond to the garbage coming out of the mouths of this type of scumbag politicians would be to dishonor the ones that have paid that ultimate price and made that ultimate sacrifice. And we're going to let somebody dictate this garbage to the American people? I don't think so! Remember her name, Senator Romero of California. Keep your eye on this scumbag! Speaking of California idiocy, California now is confiscating 10% of the people's wages in certain income brackets because of the enormous budget burden California has developed. (Source; Bill O'Reilly, Fox News Channel.)

You must be very watchful when it comes to taxes because when you see the government moving to higher and more taxation, such as BO's newly announced WAR TAX. You then know their goal is moving toward communism. Because that in part, is what communism's goal is; when government controls your money, they control you. They have you where they want you. You start becoming more and more helpless and more and more dependent on government. To head this kind of encroachment of your rights off before they get too strong of a hold on your freedoms, you must send government down the road talking to themselve's and wondering why they no longer have a job, and asking why they never were able to make things stick. Because God knows they will always come up with something to feed their voracious appetite that extends far beyond everything you possess. If you watch closely you can see these plans starting to take place. You see judges letting sex offenders go with just a slap on the wrist. That sends a stinging message to the rest of society. You see illegal aliens coming into this country and no one does anything about it and that sends a stinging message to your senses. You see Brian Doyle, who works for the Department of Homeland Security soliciting what he believes to be a 14 year-old girl for sex on the internet, and it sends a stinging message to your senses. You see Cynthia McKinney slap a Capitol Hill guard for doing his job, and that sends a stinging sensation to your senses. She looks like a voodoo doll on crack anyway, why wouldn't you stop her? You may not be able to recognize everyone on Capitol Hill, but when you once look at her, you won't soon forget her. That's a nightmare walking. When you see a judge, Judge Greer, of Pinellas County, Florida send an innocent woman, Terri Schiavo, to death by starving her to death and refusing to allow her to even have water that sends a stinging message to your senses. Please never forget her. These are just some examples of the sensory numbing messages you receive when you see a president impeached. i.e. Clinton, and never forced to leave office. These actions send a stinging message to your senses and soon you start to say, what's the use of fighting the big dog? That's the very moment you start to become a victim. That's when you start to allow your senses to succumb to the overwhelming political powers that want control. But that is in all reality when you should gather your senses about you and fight for your life. Too many times people have drowned only feet from the shore. Too many times people have burned to death only inches from the doorway. You have to learn to care and respond compassionately. You must wake the spirit within yourself that cannot be defeated. You have to know that no one has the right to control you with their agenda unless you authorize them to do so, be it government or any other enemy of your spirit or of your human or political rights. You cannot afford to allow yourself to be imprisoned by any part of an agenda of any society or government that treads on your constitutional rights and freedoms. But you, combined with all other free people of a free society, must at all cost control your government, (it's your government), and protect your precious freedom and liberties. When you pay for something, it belongs to you. You do not belong to it. You tell it what to do for you. It does not tell you what to do for it. When you start to see your representatives turning on you and attempting to take away the rights that you have paid for and what you have rights to, then you must know that you have a traitor on your hands. When you see illegal wars fought and innocent people killed and the riches of a society wasted by your elected officials, you have terrorists within your ranks. When you have people like we had with Janet Reno, who killed, murdered, the innocent people of Waco, Texas, you have a responsibility to expose, condemn, and prosecute them. You must do it. When you have a government that robs one fund, Social Security, to pay for other projects through misappropriation of funds, you know that you have a government out of control and thieves in the driver's seat of your nation. When you see an elderly gentleman being beaten by a swarm of police officers that have sworn to uphold the law as you saw in New Orleans with the elderly teacher, you have to remember the beating that happened with Rodney King in Los Angeles during the riots in Watts, California. We have to realize that nothing has changed but the faces and the names. We as people have not grown any closer to controlling our environment than we were then. American citizens still face the same abuses as before. We still face the same out of control taxation and overspending as we did in the past. We still have the politicians moving no closer to any of the goals that balance the budget. We still have the same low wages for the poor and call it a living wage. We still have the American people paying higher taxes, and we watch as the politicians continue giving themselves scheduled raises like no one else matters. They would welcome death if they had to live with the homeless and the jobless, they would welcome extinction if they had to scour the trash cans for food just so they could get through another day. Just so they could look forward to giving more and more of what they have to a government that has already robbed them of every thing they own but the very blood running through their veins. I have worked for government in a minor capacity, and I must certainly agree with Sandra Day O'Connor, former Supreme Court Justice, that legislators are more concerned about having their name on a bill than what the bill says. The waste alone would more than pay for many of the programs government says we can't afford. The real point here is we have a government we can't afford! As an example, in 2006, CNBC reported on the highest revenue grossing corporations. CNBC stated that skyrocketing energy prices propelled Exxon to the top spot, knocking Wal-Mart down to the second position on the Fortune 500 list. It was stated that Exxon raked in a $340 billion in revenue, more than a 25% increase over 2004, and had over $36 billion in profits. That is the most profit by any company or corporation in U.S. history. That's more than a 25% increase since 2004 according to CNBC and the Associated Press. Don't misunderstand what I'm talking about here. I welcome the freedom to prosper, the freedom to excel; I welcome the opportunity to succeed even beyond your wildest expectations. I believe that capitalism is a beautiful thing and unique to the American lifestyle. What I'm talking about here is stealing from the masses such as EXXON did through raising its prices during a crisis. And yet our government wants to give the oil companies hundreds of millions your tax dollars in incentives. Oil company executives have told our Congress in open forums they do not need or want that money. But our Congress gives it to them anyway. It's only tax dollars, right? Economists quote, "we used to have a market driven economy, but now we have a government-driven economy"; let me tell you friends, stand back because the shit's about to hit the fan. History has proven to us that governments have fallen, dynasties have crumbled, and most of the time in the case of oppressive and wasteful leadership. Tyrants are overcome by the people themselves. Changes are always brought about by the people, and I can tell you now that people are ready for change. But not it's this O'BUMMER type of change. They are ready with intense focus to start controlling this runaway government that has positioned itself in practically every phase of the American peoples' lives. Our government has taken it upon themselves to dictate policy where they have no authority. To literally rob its citizens in open daylight instead of holding the big oil companies accountable, our government joins forces with them by threatening to impose a windfall tax on their profits. Slick bubba, but not slick enough. Your deception is so transparent it's pathetic! This is nothing more than a merger of our government with the people who just robbed us at the pumps. It is very clear that no one is protecting the consumer. That is obvious! It is clear to the American people that the President has broken the bank. We are trillions of dollars in debt, and the American people are now coughing up $1.4 billion a day in interest alone on that debt, (that is the amount at the time of this writing.) I want to show you an example of how our leaders have continued to prolong this game of deceit. Our troops have been in conflict for a few years now and unless we use the oil in Iraq to pay for the war debt, we will be burdening the people of America and its allies much too heavily. We went there to steal their oil, so let's use it! When I went to basic training, it took me eight weeks to complete the basic training course and then I went directly into active status. Now after three years the Iraqi forces are still not ready to stand on their own as an army? Somebody here is full of crap! Don't try to push that down the throats of the American people. Is it any wonder that 81% of Americans now believe the Bush administration was a complete and total failure? If you've never questioned authority or your elected officials that are supposed to be running this dog and pony government for you, then I would strongly urge you to get ready because you are going to have to make a decision. And now that BO is at the helm, you're going to see spending like you've never seen before. The politicians have no standard by which they operate, and obviously no shame. We have a predator government and now because of its indignant self-indulgent and self-serving agenda, along with its political and philosophical stance, it is easily identified. This government is looking to burden you for more and more support in the way of your tax dollars - whether by direct tax, indirect tax or by inflation. The republicans will do nothing to stop the democrats' reckless race to destruction because they know that you will blame the democrats for the terrible shape we're in. Neither party gives a damn about what you really think, you're just a pawn. You stupid taxpayer, you shouldn't even voice your opinion except in some remote little circle down at the Dairy Queen where nothing ever gets done but the rehashing of your political views and opinions to anyone who will listen. This government thinks that's about as far as it will go, yet stronger men and women have risen from the ashes of this kind of destructive circumstance to become champions of our society. They have accomplished miraculous recovery when they realized their ship was slowly sinking, and as a last result began to arm themselves against an oppressive government and the self-appointed, out of control executioners. Arm yourself with knowledge of the political past and present, arm yourself by aligning yourself with other parties and groups of people who have had enough of this kind of government greed and out of control dominance now dictating every part of your life. Go to the internet and view the website www.freedomtofascism.com again. I have to return to this website for a little enlightenment and stimulation now and then. We know we had a government of complete losers with the Bush administrations wasteful, brainless, spineless, embarrassing, do-nothing dorks! But somebody has to pay for these illegal wars and the debts that government creates and then so conveniently hands over to the people to settle even after you have already paid for every weapon, tank, airplane, ship and loss of life plus the rebuilding of your enemies' countries. I personally would like to see the entire elected official lot imprisoned or put in front of a firing squad. Senator Frist, of Tennessee admitted openly on the Bill O'Reilly show, that in 1986, the government had an opportunity to curtail this illegal immigration run for the border crap that has now impacted the entire United States. But this government failed to do their job again. And again, this current situation is the result of this out of touch, lazy crooked congress. I think there is something much larger going on with all this illegal immigration however. Before leaving office, President Bush's approval ratings continued to plummet, and still there continues to be more and more accusations of illegal wiretapping and surveillance on the American public; why the American public? Sounds like political paranoia to me. What is it that they have to hide, as if we didn't know? Charts of our budget show that we were in surplus before President, scumbag Bush took office and now not only do we no longer have a surplus, but we are in the red by trillions of dollars. And again, let me stress that as of April 6, 2008, we continue paying $1.4 billion a day in interest just on our debt. The oil companies have ripped the American public off by the hundreds of millions of dollars at the pumps, and yet the tax breaks and largesse given them by our government seems to never end. The price per gallon of gasoline is however only 12 cents a gallon in Venezuela, while we continue reaching deeper into our pockets to try to come up with $3.00 per gallon in the United States. And, MY GOD, Europe is paying over $8.00 PER GALLON! We rescued Iraq from a tyrant, but we can't use any of the Iraqi oil to help pay for the cost of the war and for the rebuilding of their nation. We not only have stupid politicians, we have some of the dumbest businessmen in existence! One in the same, might I add.

Let me get your opinion on this. If you were the government, I mean our government; wouldn't you have made preparations for the oil crisis that the U.S. faced recently? A simpleton can imagine that if we were to produce alternative fuels, the price of oil would drop to less than half of what it is today, resulting in gas prices about half of what they are currently. As of the writing of this book, we could drill off the coast of Mexico, we could drill in Alaska, and we could drill in Texas, or open up the existing wells in Texas that the government so conveniently capped a few years ago. Don't tell me that the government didn't know what was coming. This was all by design. But why, and who made it happen?

Have we been so asleep in this nation that anything can happen and no one understands or responds? Are we so willing to be taken over and controlled like puppets? May 15, 2008, President Bush's address to the nation was a splendid few minutes of garbage and absolute stupidity, contrived and shallow; empty and meaningless, hollow and without compassion. Can you gather that I was not impressed? As was the majority of the nation might I add. I'm not the only one in this nation that is disgusted with these fat-cat do nothing bums in Washington. There are countless credible politicians that can't break through the closed doors and political gridlock as well. The Bush administration was a joke of the worst kind. In his last term he made sure he left this country crippled financially and so in debt that it will take years to recover. But the cost won't be coming out of his pocket, because there are people like you and me. And we're going to do what we've always done. We're going to clean up after these selfish greedy spoiled little mama's boys who walk away from their responsibility and espouse so eloquently as only in grand Bush/Cheney and now newcomer Obama style, to the entire world convincingly, they've done a good job. Nothing could be further from the truth! If you really want to know what has devastated our economy and sent us into a tailspin causing devastating home foreclosures and job losses, then look no further than your own government. The only reason that Bush mentioned the border problem before he left office was to protect his party who was scrambling to keep their seats. He certainly didn't do his party any favors when he addressed the nation in the latter part of 2008; if you can call that a speech. It was laughable at best and so to the point that there are rumors of many people switching political parties because of it. I think I would investigate other political avenues, not necessarily Republican or Democrat. However, something has to be done for sure because both parties are cancerous and terminally ill. We as a country must point out to this government that they have become dangerously obese and cannot function by continuing to deplete the human populace of more and more of our political and strategic resources. Enough is enough! Ask yourself this question, why hasn't anyone done anything about our out-of-control federal government's outright thievery of the American people's money with items like the alternative minimum tax? These are not our representatives. These are our enemies who develop this crap and vote to pass it into law. If anyone should go to prison, it should be these lowlife outright thieves. The only way anything is ever going to change for the better is for us, the American people, to organize and overwhelmingly, strategically, meticulously and instantaneously take back our government! But it will never happen as long as we stay separated and indecisive in the collective decisions to streamline effective policy. It makes me think how unorganized and unfocused we are and that we are no more intelligent than those running our present government. We stand on a line of indecision and fail to produce any real results because we run helter-skelter trying to put out all the other little fires that keep us off balance. I do have to applaud Governor Arnold Schwarzenegger at this point though. I realize this statement may be a mistake in judgment on my part so early in his administration. But he recently condemned the congress for failing to cross party lines to come together as a body to focus on the state of California's budget dilemma - but one that the government obviously created, and for which is obviously to blame and responsible. (December 2008). As he stated, they, the congress, have done nothing to curtail spending. Maybe this is just a cover-your-ass strategy, but he certainly nailed this one. However, that is not only a problem in California with state government; it's a major problem nationally. Headline news also in Illinois with the governor there. Just another scumbag phony politician with his hand in the cookie jar and his ass caught in a trap. People, something has to be done even if it means drastic measures. "And you can use your own imagination here", as stated by Rod Blagojevich - a Donald Trump want-to-be. With "the hair", he and his wife could both go down for this garbage. My personal take on this is, if Governor Blagojevich is convicted on all these charges and especially on trying to sell the senate seat vacated by president elect BO, then all of those bidding for the senate seat should be summoned for questioning as well. I'm hopeful that this will not be overlooked. As Einstein said, insanity is doing the same thing over and over and expecting a different result. It just sickens me though to hear these politicians repeat themselves in their analytical tone of voice as if they were going to look into anything with any seriousness of commitment to change anything or accomplish anything except searching for newer ways to take more of our money for some other bridge to nowhere, or build another hundred million dollar computer system that doesn't work so they scrap it with the attitude that it was only $100 million. Tax money was all that it was. Yet over and over they continue to repeat themselves and expect a different result. They continue to apply the same old used bandages to new wounds. And now they're asking even more stupid questions - questions that even kindergartners could get right. (A) Should English be the official language of the United States? Well, let's do some comparisons. Has English ever been the official language of the United States? Should Chinese be the official language of China? Or should Japanese be the official language of Japan? How about Italian for Italy? Or Spanish for Mexico; and you have to ask if English should be the official language of the United States? Every day you wake to a different plan by the federal government attempting to confuse or take away another right that you have. At first it's some of the things that the Fed is trying to take away that don't seem to be that important until you investigate the real impact it would have on the society as a whole. For instance, the federal government now wants to take away the attorney client privilege. That is one of the last rights you have as an American citizen before you are living in a dictatorship society. But that attempt is not only being made here, governments around the world are all attempting the same types of rights reversal. Pay attention, your freedom is at risk. When you have no rights to an attorney, and judges can hand down sentences without reprisal, or there is no client attorney privilege, you are in trouble because you have no protection then from a rogue government. As much as we like to condemn attorneys, they are a necessary evil. We would be making a grave mistake to allow our government to get away with this gross injustice. The very freedoms that our military is fighting for to protect other countries is being purposely and obviously eroded right here in the United States. As our American men and women fight to bring freedom to others, our own government is trying to rob the American people of theirs! We all know that politicians

124

are lowlifes, thieves, and self-serving liars. Rather than honest committed people elected to serve society, we have educated idiots. They ask the American people to elect them. They ask the American people to give them their prestigious jobs, they take an oath to uphold the Constitution of the United States and represent the people of this country. Yet we know that they have endorsed and passed laws giving our competitors the edge, giving America's competitors the best or better advantage when it comes to fair trade, failing to protect this country's borders, failing to communicate agency to agency within our own departments of security which results in why we are in this lopsided trade deficit. They are morally and ethically stupid. Can you grasp any reality or make any sense out of this governmental quagmire at this point? We have a cloud of confusion hanging over this nation; it seems no one can come to a clear decision over anything. It's either racist or profiling or politically incorrect to act any other way than the way these losers are acting, and that my friends in part, is what cost the Fort Hood Army personnel their wounds as well as their lives. I stand firmly on the belief that if you don't know who you are or what you stand for, you are going to have one hell of a time convincing me that you're the person for the job or that your agenda makes any sense or merits any attention especially when it comes to writing and implementing the law. We have lobbyists that are cancerous to our leadership because our leadership in all reality is a group of addicts. Lobbyists know how addicted our politicians are to their money. They just dangle a few dollars in front of these representatives and they bite like blinded fish. There is sucker bait everywhere. And when they get caught, they scream unconstitutional, or oh, I've been so deprived all my life I had a bad childhood, I grew up in a bad environment, I have no self-esteem, all the school kids made fun of me. Well, all that tells me is that your parents were stupid, too. Listen, why is it that even kids can detect a loser and adults can't? Because kids know instinctively who is rotten. Here we are with all of our higher degrees, and we can't read a loser with a magnifying glass. When we do spot a loser we don't say anything because we don't want to make waves. Well friends, I'm from the old school, and I calls 'em like I sees 'em! Authority means nothing to me if it's misguided or misrepresented by someone who has lost all sense of reality and direction while trying to enforce authority. It's like one comedian said, "watching a politician operate is like watching a fat drunk man try to cross an icy road." But this is a new day and a new time. From here on out we must be loud, be vocal, and be on top of the issues. We need to apply the pressure to those who try to escape their responsibilities.

If you're going to take our money for your salaries in the form of tax, then you're going to do your fucking job! The job that you asked for... no excuses... end of discussion... period!!! You have a responsibility to your position and you have a responsibility to your boss. And right now the American people are still your boss. The American people are the people that pay for your lifestyle so you can send your children to college. The American people will judge you harshly, starting right now, and not sometime in the distant future or when it's convenient. We the American people must adopt a no tolerance platform. Get hold of that mindset and lock in on it and commit to raising hell when politicians break the rules or get caught with their hands in your pocket, or sell their office for personal gain. This type of separation of powers between the government and the people doesn't give you the right to break the laws any more than it does the thieves at Enron, or William 'THIEF CONGRESSMAN' Jefferson. If you want to sell out the American people, go ahead, but don't cry foul when we catch a rotten ass. We the people are taking back what we have the right to. What the American people are telling you is, we are on the scent of a lot of dishonest, lying, deceiving scum in our house. Maybe we need to check the freezer compartments of more of Capitol Hill's finest. Don't look to the party to defend you because the party will not save you. The party will let you down just as it has let the American people down. Nowadays, the party is made up of those who are in politics to serve those who are as corrupt as themselves. There might be safety in numbers at times; however, the smart and innovative ones will always rise through the ranks once focus and vision, coupled with the moral compass are in place. It would be in your best interest to pick up a copy of Judge Napolitano's book "The Constitution in Exile", and read it over and over and over until it is clear in your mind what is happening to our freedoms and our constitutional rights. Maybe then you will feel the same fire that I feel in my core, and understand what opportunists our government officials have become. I see a push to control the American population like never before by this government. Our government will use tactics like 9/11 and the Fort Hood massacre to get you to turn your attention to the confusion while they sneak their agenda through. This 'same shit different day' political crap is going to stop once and for all.

The Patriot Act is a plot to rob you of even more of your freedoms. Ask those who have signed the Patriot Act if they even looked at it or read it? How many politicians put their signature to the Patriot Act before they looked at it? When George W. signed the Patriot Act into law, he became the American's #1 enemy. While you are focused on what the government is doing and going to do to protect you, they are plotting to enslave you with the passage of some other agenda. You have no freedoms left. You may think you do but every day the sun rises there are those on Capitol Hill laying plans to trap you like rabbits. Don't ever give up your guns, never, never … you had better pay attention now. According to judge Napolitano's book, "The Constitution in Exile", the Patriot Act downright robs you of your constitutional rights to free speech, robs you of your own self defense when you have not committed a crime, robs you of your free speech to discuss the matter with any friends or family, and threatens you with prison time if you do. It gives local police the authority to write their own warrants and bypasses former procedures of obtaining a judge's approval and signature for such acts. So much for free speech and due process, huh? Do you think that governmental investigative departments need approval to obtain information from your bank? Do you think that they need approval to obtain information from your electric company to gather information about you? From what else do you think you're protected? They can extract information from your computer. They can go to your place of employment and tell your boss to keep his mouth shut about what they're doing! How about your doctor and your medical history? They can access your financial records and tell the bank officers to button up about it. Heard enough? That's just the beginning. Politicians will stop at nothing to further their agenda, and they will sell you out for any amount of money for a chance at power or an opportunity to bring attention to themselves through any law they feel would give them the edge over you - such is the case of BO and the health care system.

Sixty-eight percent of the American people do not want government-controlled health care as the polls clearly state, yet BO continues to push against the American people's wishes. That is dictatorship. I don't care what the cause. If you don't wake up to reality now, you will find yourselves enslaved, more controlled with no constitutional rights and no bill of rights when you do finally wake up. The founding fathers would die of shock if they saw what the greed mongers and the federal communist minded dictator types have done to the constitution that they fought and died for. It's no wonder that people are saying we need a third party. While I don't believe that we need a third party, I do believe that we need a party that does the will of the people. Having a third party would only grow government larger, and we already have too much garbage on the hill at present. Having a third party would be like trying to herd kittens. A third party is not necessary. What we have to do is clean house. We don't need to destroy the structure we have in place, just replace the inhabitants and their cancerous contents, revive the constitution and deliver the power the back to the owners of this country. We need to remove the trash that is blocking the passage ways, put federal government on notice as you hand them written documentation to vacate the buildings immediately. They no longer have a job. OUT! Therefore, taking the power and the money away from the federal government and making the heads of each state responsible to the people of those states. THE FEDERAL GOVERNMENT IS GONE. They have done nothing but cause chaos, waste resources, and destroy our hopes of ever being on any kind of stable foundation, and yet, still they try and convince you, me and the rest of America that they are indispensable. What we need to do is eliminate the electorate and get back to the popular vote, and destroy the IRS and the Federal Reserve. In doing so, we will return the power to the people. However; that is only the first step we need to take as a people in a free society. We must limit government in almost everything except protecting this country in time of attack or invasion from alien forces. Our politicians, our leadership, are guilty and the cause of the wars we have had to fight in the past. You will never have any real freedom as long as the government is dictating every move you can make. This has to be eliminated. The newly appointed government at this point would have to request permission to spend your money. Not like it is now. What happens now is state governments send collected taxes to the federal government, and when the states need it back for whatever reason, the states must then ask for it. How damned stupid is that? Our borders would not be vulnerable to the point they are today because we would know when to act and what to do. We would not wait on an obese, half asleep, un-American federal agency to sign off on something they haven't read, don't understand or don't care to understand. Unlike the federal government, we as a people don't have our heads up our rectum. We have a pattern of what not to do just by looking at the mess the federal government has made with our liberties, our financial freedoms, and our welfare. We have politicians that vote to go to war and then condemn our troops and charge them with murder when they defend themselves. For every enemy they kill, they should be given a medal. If in fact it is a legal war, unlike Iraq, Vietnam, and Pearl Harbor, or the War Between the States for that matter. The purpose of the battle and war is to win the conflict. Not to make the international bankers rich. It's like former President Ronald Reagan said, "it's easy to determine the outcome of a war, we win, they loose, next case!" We put our troops on the ground and expect them not to shoot when they are being shot at. What fool thought of that one? Put his phony ass out there and give him or her, an empty gun. Instant diarrhea! These are the fools that have gotten us so far into debt that future generations will be paying off the debt long after our life has ended! And the sad part is that your children and my children will grow up absorbing the burden that NOT WE, but with what THIS GOVERNMENT has burdened them. Our representatives have written so many laws to enslave us, that they now are caught in their own net. We have enemy combatants that we have to take to court! We have illegal aliens that now dictate to us what we must do to enable them and grant them benefits even though they are here in this country illegally and with false documents. Yet our government looks at this as frivolous or unimportant. They give credence and allow these illegalities because of the many self entangling laws they have written and are unable to use to manipulate in their favor, therefore, handing over to our enemy the legal use of America's justice system. How stupid, how utterly stupid; but only if you take this at face value. This is a plan - a plan conceived by leaders in our present government. Eric Holder, Attorney General, obviously taking orders from his Muslim friend and President of the United States, BO, to allow the trials of the accused 9/11 terrorists to take place in the United States court system and not in the military courts. Here is where you must STOP and connect the dots. We have a President elected from the most politically corrupt city in America and his first official act is ordering Gitmo closed making sure the TERRORISTS rights are not abused. And then this stupid congress rushes in to elect our President's good friend Eric Holder, whose law firm is representing 17 of those Gitmo terrorists! AMERICA, YOU MUST REALIZE THIS, IF THESE SELF ADMITTED TERRORISTS CAN USE THE COURTS IN THIS MANNER WITH THE HELP OF OUR BELOVED GOVERNMENT IDIOT OFFICIALS, A TECHNICALITY COULD SET THE ACCUSED FREE! We have an Attorney General who is introducing and authorizing this procedure, while defending his stance in this matter. Remember his name - ERIC HOLDER. You can deal with him later.

In a time of outlaw government coming into view such as what we have presently, only the brave will survive. And as always, the ones who have their assets fully protected and in abundance will rise to the heights of success, just like in the great depression. But I'm afraid the rest of America will continue to follow the leaders blindly into ruin and never recover from fools like George W. Bush or Barack Obama. If you can't yet see the shaping of this country taking place, then just hold what you've got and stay with me. While America is becoming an aggressor nation that everyone hates and no one trusts any longer, the Federal Reserve is pulling the rug out from under the American people by manipulating and destroying America's monetary system. It's a perfect time for a junior senator puppet like BO, with no real track record to do battle with those whom have been planning for this day to come for years. All eyes are upon us and for once the black race will temporarily be allowed to shine. But when BO screws it up and is unable to sustain and clean up the Bush administration's mess, he will set not only America but the black race back a hundred years because the entire system and the American way of life will start to collapse according to plan. This could be a defining moment in history for America. But you must realize that also this moment in our history of having an African-American president sends a message to the rest of the African-American community. There will no longer be the excuse that "ooh I can't get a job because I'm black"! Or, "I don't stand a chance because I am an African-American", will not be accepted as even the slightest excuse. Over the last few decades I have seen the black race given more opportunity than anyone else, more than any other race. I've seen the rise of talent of all ages in the black race. You have some real winners out there in the sports field, the music industry, in politics, and in the business world. So don't be like an O.J. or a Marion Barry. If you're going to fight to win, don't destroy it when you get there! When you arrive, don't be like Whitney Houston, fall victim to drugs and almost destroy the most beautiful voice ever heard. Be an example that future generations will respect, love, and honor and hold in high esteem. How about a little self respect! Don't be like George W. Bush, Condi Rice, or Dick Cheney - The Three Stooges of politics, be somebody! The whole world is watching!

We are facing trillion's in deficit spending, yet we are christening ships honoring Herbert Walker Bush. Are you about to vomit yet? When you add the following components, Social Security, Medicaid, the cost of the Iraq war, the interest on the national debt, the bailouts of the financial markets nearing $30 Billion, AIG over $150 billion, FANNIE MAE and FREDDIE MAC $200 billion, AUTO INDUSTRY $25 billion, ECONOMIC STIMULUS nearing $170 billion, MONEY MARKET GUARANTEES OVER $650 billion, THE TERM AUCTION FACILITY OVER $1.5 trillion, COMMERCIAL PAPER FUNDING OVER $1.3 trillion, FDIC TEMPORARY LIQUIDITY GUARANTEE $$ UNLIMITED!!! FOREIGN EXCHANGE SWAPS, $$ UNLIMITED!!! You're going to be devastated financially if this kind of chaos continues. This economy will collapse! According to a CNN broadcast on January 11, 2009, when we reach the projected number of $50 trillion, this nation will have fallen like the Roman Empire fell. And it will have fallen from the inside! October 14, 2008, the national debt clock in New York runs out of digit space. Lou Dobbs states that our leaders have squandered our wealth!!! In an interview

138

someone asked President Bush what he felt about the economic downturn and he responded with, "you are going to have to ask an economist". WHAT? WAIT JUST A MINUTE GEORGIE BOY. You're not off the hook that easy. Wasn't it you who started all this and kept pushing for the multi billion dollar stimulus bail out packages? HUH? Wasn't it? When someone said the United States is the land of opportunity, a place where you can be anything you want to be, I don't think they knew George W. was listening. To bad you can't take some things you say back! Now that he, GEORGIE BOY, is out of there, the better off all of America will be. BO, however, is concerned about where to send the prisoners of Guantanamo Bay, Cuba. What could be more appropriate than sending them to live on the Bush ranch in Crawford, Texas? I believe that once the smell is out of the white house and the dust settles somewhat you will see an avalanche of charges brought against old George W. I HAVE ABSOLUTELY NO RESPECT FOR THE FUCK! He did more to steal your rights and destroy your freedoms by enacting the Patriot Act than you will ever imagine. He was never my President; and if you'll dig deep enough, you'll find he was never your President either. He attacked a country – Iraq, who had no weapons of mass destruction, who didn't have a chance in hell of protecting itself, had no Navy, and no Air Force. Iraq had no war chest whereby money was available to take on a superpower like America. George W. Bush is a coward who stood aboard the USS Abraham Lincoln aircraft carrier and announced to the world, MISSION ACCOMPLISHED! How arrogant and how despicably embarrassing. When you've finished reading this book, pick up a copy of "The Dark Side" by Jane Meyer, published by Double Day. You will start to get a clearer picture of BULLSHIT BUSH!!!

Listen, you have to be very careful putting your trust in your candidate when you don't know them very well. You just can't give your trust and support to people who stand there and make promises that sound good or that relate to your wishes. Benjamin Franklin said, "They that give up essential liberty for a little temporary safety deserves neither liberty nor safety". This present government attempts to chip away at your constitutional rights and freedoms all the time. These are not the people you want running your government. You want people protecting your rights and freedoms.

You want people who understand the price paid by those who originally fought hard and long and with great sacrifice to keep freedom alive. Let me pass along some profound information that a friend of mine shared with me in January 2009……..."The democracy will cease to exist when you take away from those who are willing to work and give to those who would not" - by Thomas Jefferson. Keep your eye on BO and his ACORN associates, his charitable bail out of everybody and their cousins with your money.

Here are some words of wisdom to ponder:
"It is incumbent on every generation to pay for its own debts as it goes. A principle which if acted upon would save one half the wars of the world." Thomas Jefferson.
"I predict happiness for Americans if they can prevent the government from wasting the labors of the people under the pretense of taking care of them." Thomas Jefferson.
"My reading of history convinces me that most bad government comes from too much government." Thomas Jefferson.
"No free man will ever be debarred the use of arms." Thomas Jefferson.

This is a major concern of BO, who ultimately wants to control firearms and ammunition by raising taxes on this constitutional American right. Research HR47. BO wants to raise taxes on ammunition by 400% to 500% and laser number each projectile. Sounds like more paranoia at first thought.

Let's continue with more wisdom:

"The strongest reason for people to retain the right to keep and bear arms is, as a last resort, to protect themselves against tyranny in government." Thomas Jefferson.

"The tree of liberty must be refreshed from time to time with the blood of patriots and tyrants." Thomas Jefferson.

GRASP THE FOLLOWING, AND THEN TELL ME YOU ARE VOLUNTEERING YOUR TAXES AS THE CONSTITUTION SO EXPRESSES.

"To compel a man to subsidize with his taxes the propagation of ideas which he disbelieves and abhors is sinful and tyrannical." Thomas Jefferson.

I SAY THAT THE IRS IS GUILTY OF EXTORTION. I SAY THAT THE USE OF THE CITIZENS' MONEY INCLUDED IN THE HEALTH CARE BILL UNDER SUSPICION FOR THE USE OF ELECTIVE ABORTION IS REASON ENOUGH FOR TAX REVOLT AND REVOLUTION.

In the light of our present financial state, it's profound that Thomas Jefferson made the above statements in the year 1802. This is how long you have been robbed by this government. It is time we got serious.

"I believe that banking institutions are more dangerous to our liberties than standing armies. If the American people ever allow private banks to control the issue of their currency, first by inflation, then by deflation, (i.e. FEDERAL RESERVE), the banks and corporations that will grow up around the banks will deprive the people of all the property until their children wake up homeless on the continent their fathers conquered." Thomas Jefferson.

Thanks to our elected senator and traitor, Nelson Aldrich, that's just what happened. And we were warned as far back as the early 1800's.

So this scumbag political deception and robbing the American laborer is not a new concept. This has been going on for centuries. Are you about ready to start taking action? Then stay with me,

Thomas Jefferson
1743 - 1826

Our financial problems were started, and are always caused by our own government officials, with the Federal Reserve being at the very top of the list.

Bullshit Bush left office on January 20, 2009. He should run and hide his ugly face from society and never again utter a word that would make the decent people of this country remember he ever existed. He is the most despicable human that ever took a breath; other than Hitler himself. Yet he continues a family tradition from father, "Read My Lips", Herbert Walker Bush to banker Grandfather and traitor, Prescott Bush, who helped support Hitler's war through his banking connections. To confirm this statement just research Prescott Bush.

Now, on to the other problems we face financially because of a government that just won't keep its hands off of the money and markets that would recover all by themselves if left alone to do so. Believe me when I tell you, this financial crisis America in facing will only benefit the financial institutions considered too large to fail. Government will control the money markets like never before regardless of what change BO says he wants to bring to the country. You and I, and all free Americans are doomed to see this country move toward a socialistic society! Our financial woes started with government, and we have been paying the price ever since, which brings me to the Federal Reserve System again. It is a system that should have never been put into place or established because its main purpose is, was and has been meant to be, to enslave the people of this country since its beginning. It has given control of our monetary systems to banking. It has allowed them to print and charge an interest on the very money we owned and had the right to control ourselves. Again, our biggest and most dangerous financial enemy lives among us and every day determines our perpetual monetary success or failure. But then we had a traitor or two in our midst who were our own elected officials, thanks to Senator Nelson Aldrich, who in 1913 developed this underhanded banking cartel and pushed this agreement through so that Woodrow Wilson, who was to become president would sign it into law. The agreement that was pushed through and became law was drafted by BANKERS, not our government! Two days before Christmas, when most everyone was home for Christmas vacation, they called for a vote, and their evil scheme became law. Later President Wilson apologized. The reason that I make this point is to alert the American public to the fact that all this attention and the federal bailout bullshit is just another scheme to take your attention off the underlying plan that is going to enslave you further. You must know by now that no government, unless socialistic or communist, takes from one part of society to give to another. As analyst Jim Rogers said in Congressman Ron Paul's book "The Revolution", on page 261, "by the bail out of Freddie Mac and Fannie Mae, America has already become more communist than red China." In other words, take from the tax payer to bail out corporate failure!! We all make mistakes, not only in times of war but in times of peace.

But I believe that the most critical mistake we are making is of and by ourselves for not holding government's feet to the fire and controlling their movement by rigorous standard. Our present government is full of self serving thieves, liars and outright criminals, and yet, it always has been. It is just a matter of time until we see a democracy that has no resemblance to the past and the proud self-respecting, God-fearing men and women that once represented America. The power of government is in the wrong hands! I also think that deep down inside all of us, we must think that if we don't make waves the problems will somehow magically just disappear, a knight in shining armor will ride in and rescue all of us and we will all live happily ever after. No, you and I will forever be responsible for the choices we make or don't make today. By allowing government to make choices for us that are in direct opposition to our core belief is the reason we have what we have today. Because no one made waves to stop what we had yesterday, is why we are suffering the consequences today. Whether you agree with me or not, the fact remains that we allow government to pass laws that kill innocent babies by abortion, start illegal wars that murder innocent unsuspecting people and waste resources, disrupt environments, and extract finances from people through taxes (extortion). Just because governments pass laws that say it is legal does not make it morally or constitutionally so!!!! The Patriot Act is a prime example. President BO stated that he taught constitutional law. So, when he reviews the Patriot Act, with a stroke of a pen he could erase any unconstitutional content and reverse the law that is counter to the American wishes. What the hell are you waiting on BO? The list goes on and on. The American people have waited all we're going to my oratory friend. This is not my government any longer! My government would have a clear vision and moral judgment and a common sense commitment to do no harm! To protect the innocent! To help the helpless! We need to be ashamed of ourselves! We have, through time and lack of control of our government, placed faith and trust in those incapable of running government with any focus or moral compass. They are drunk on their own power and self indulgence; living only for today, and running aground at every turn for lack of vision. We are doomed to make the same dreadful mistakes again and again! We have been slowly slipping into a self induced coma of irreversible consequence. And I had hoped as President BO promised, change, and a commitment to excellence, to right the absurd wrong that has ruled for too long, a clean break as he stated, from business as usual in Washington. But that is yet to be seen.

I have waited the hundred days to write any more and to give President BO an opportunity to get his act together and now that time is up. I will now continue with this book. Where does he stand with me on a scale of one to ten? Simple - HE SUCKS!!! Off of the chart. Not even a good hustler. He is a big mouth in an empty suit. Anyone who would agree that it is okay to kill innocent unborn babies through late term abortion is as guilty as George W. Bush's illegal murderous Iraq War. He is a socialist and has committed tremendous mistakes by stealing your constitutional rights from you and me by disallowing us the right to vote before taking our tax money and bailing out private institutions. That is a breech of our constitutional rights. By this act alone, BO has assumed the position of dictator and should immediately be impeached!!! He taught constitutional law for years? Then he just proved to me when he gave your money to the financial institutions without any approval passed by a vote by and of the people, he destroyed his own credibility. In order for this to be legal, our permission is required by vote. Look, government wants you to depend totally on them, and when you do, they will have total control of you. They want to control you, the financial institutions, taxation, and any free market movement. That in part, is how and why you have no control presently in this government. They took your tax money and bailed out the failing financial institutions. They control transportation; they control the air waves, FCC, radio and TV, etc. They control air travel; they control ocean travel. Eventually, like China, they will tell you how many children you can have and what kind of cars you can drive or own!! It will get worse. Just how long will we continue to follow the brainless down the road to self destruction? How can we respect our elected officials when we see them bow before foreign leaders announcing to the world that we are not a Christian nation? It is abortion today for the innocent and helpless, and end of life at the hand of government for the weak and elderly tomorrow. BO, sure as hell does not represent me or you for that matter. What do we have on our hands? What do we know about our own President? That is a frightening thought!!! What have we done? Who is this that represents this great country? We keep putting the same types of people in official charge and expecting different results. BO can't command the military. He knows nothing of the military history. He is like Clinton, and yet, worse than Bush. Do we not consider all of this when someone attempts to take control of America as leader or as President? This is insanity!! It would be the same as if no one voted at future elections. What would happen if no one showed up to vote? If not one vote were cast. That would either be the beginning of rebuilding America or all of our problems would be over because all of the low lifes in our capitol would possibly kill each other fighting for what they claimed was their rightful post, when it is likely that none of them can describe their own departmental responsibility as it is. They certainly can't explain to my satisfaction what is in half of the bills they pass! And especially our health care bill. This health care bill is absolute suicide to the American people. This is insanity, and we had better come against this with a unified force that is loud and clear, determined and most certainly unstoppable. Now, there can be no mistake in what I mean. If it doesn't serve the will of the people, if it doesn't serve equally all Americans, if it doesn't serve all Americans better than what we have now, then why are we wasting our time? What is the reason that government would want to get involved with the health care system, or to control it? What is the rush to pass the bill they have drafted and haven't read? This is just another smoke screen, no? I have seen losers like this in the work force. They walk around with a clipboard appearing to be in a hurry, darting in and out of corridors speaking only to those who are their superiors, and then they are gone again. They are the first ones to go to lunch, the first ones in line on Friday to pick up their check and the first ones to snitch you out if something goes wrong on your watch. They are the first ones to offer a solution for a problem which in most cases is a long line of drawn out garbled bullshit! And then, like BO, who wants to tax your ass if you make over a certain amount of money every year. Do you ever wonder why there are more and more offshore corporations that absolutely refuse to pay any tax to the fucked up government coffers so the government can spend, waste and tax some more! The mentality of these idiots is going to cause the American people to revolt, and when it happens this time there won't just be tea in the harbor, there will be BLOOD IN THE STREETS!!! These creepy little blood suckers will deny that they ever worked for the government or the IRS. Also rumored, is that BO will continue former President Bush's North American treaty agreement with Canada and Mexico. The American people need to stop right now and lift their noses up from the grind stone and start to take their government back by whatever means, and without hesitation. Just do a 360° turn real slowly with your eyes open and take a glimpse of the governments all over the world closing in on the people. EVERY ONE THAT I HAVE TALKED TO REGARDING THEIR GOVERNMENT IN THE LAST FIVE YEARS IS BEGINNING TO GET THIS DISGUSTING GLIMPSE OF WHAT IS EVOLVING. What the politicians have in mind is really nothing new. It's the same mindset that called for the extinction of the Native American Indian!! Only it's YOU this time!! It's the same thing that cost six million Jews their lives only it's happening to YOU this time!! It's the same that happened under HITLER, POL POT, MUSSOLINI,

SADAM HUSSEIN, and its happening to YOU this time. Did I forget to mention, it's the same thing that happened under former President G.W. Bush, which stands for 'God-damned Worthless Butcher'. Now it's happening under BO, and it's you that it's happening to this time. Your freedom, your liberty, and your independence have been stolen, your financial independence embezzled through this country's incompetent leadership. It isn't enough to try and take everything you own through forced government programs, but even in death, they want all that you have ever accomplished; they want all your assets, your estate, everything. Nothing has really changed; the only difference you see in the blood suckers of today is they are wearing suits, driving cars, and talking on cell phones instead of riding horses and yelling through megaphones. Your extinction is of no concern as long as they accomplish their goals. They would serve any government as long as it would benefit their political aspirations. They would salute any flag if it meant they could be a part of the ruling class. They have no allegiance to anyone or anything of quality. Their counterparts whom have attempted this kind of maneuver in past history have all ended up dead by the hand of those they tried to accommodate.

I may seem to be redundant at times but I dare not apologize, because I know what I must do to keep the fire lit in your soul and your mind focused until you, on your own, pick up the torch and spread the word of warning to others that EVERYTHING, is on the line. Right now I look at BO and his minions in an attempt to impose a war tax on the people to accomplish government's gruesome tasks in these illegal wars, to tax the ammunition for fire arms 400% to 500% and laser print every projectile so that the government will know where the expelled ammo came from and who purchased it. You will of course be required to sign for your ammo. As I've said before, sounds like panic in our officials. Well, well, well, but look out for this one coming down the line. Its senate bill SB-2009. It is pending, but if passed, it will require you to put on your 1040 tax form all the guns that you own, and may require you to be finger printed as well. HELLO! This is an amendment to the internal act of 1986, and means that the finance committee can pass this one without the senate voting on it at all. You can find more information by going to www.Senate.gov. You can find the bill by doing a search by the bill number, SB-2009. THIS IS A BACK DOOR GUN

REGISTRATION. And it requires attention by everyone who is determined to keep their firearm freedoms in this country. I hope that you are starting to believe me and are listening to what I'm trying to tell you. You are in for the fight of your life!!! I mean that literally!!! A war tax; the people already paid for every stinking dime of every war ever fought. I think what we are experiencing here is the boiling the frog theory. In effect what this does is make you so weak by imposing more and more on you that you eventually collapse under the weight of the load. First you put a frog in a pan of cool water and slowly increase the heat over a period of time. The slow heating of the water weakens the frog's ability to reject or escape what is happening until it is too late, and the frog becomes helpless and is eventually overcome to the point that it, (you in this case) cannot resist. This is happening to us now.

A perfect example is the following few lines: Pat Buchanan; former speech writer for Presidents Regan and Nixon, and co-host of the television show Crossfire, brought to light that over $53 billion dollars would be saved in filling out tax (EXTORTION) forms alone. And all the money you earned would go home with you instead of to the IRS parasites. All illegal aliens would contribute to the economy, and those who participate in illegal activity would not escape. Only dictators, rulers and rogue governments threaten their populations with unwarranted taxation (EXTORTION). As we well know, there is vast knowledge and proof of such in our government. When this all ends up exposed and in court, we have overwhelming proof that this government is guilty of fraud, extortion, embezzlement, misappropriation of funds, numerous human rights violations; not to mention numerous constitutional breaches. If Presidents, elected officials and government as a whole won't respect common rules of law, then that pretty much leaves you and me to go forward with developing our own agenda and forcing them into the courts by whatever means. U.S. District Judge Anna Digs Taylor ruled that President Bush overstepped his constitutional authority attempting to give himself unfettered control to go to war with Iraq and to impose illegal torture procedure on the captives. Now I want to see where that leaves BO. But for now, BO is seeking a rule that stops this out of control spending. What? Well, there's always suicide bubba, or worse, maybe having to listen to a little more advice from former President Bush, since he's the one that handed you the baton in this race to destroy America!!! But then we all know government is the dumbest animal in the barn anyway. You and I both know that government is only good at a couple of things and that is hype, taxing, spending, cover-up, murder and bullshit. You have to realize that this group of false prophets - Republicans, Democrats and Indies - are all just puppets in the grand scheme of things, acting in concert because of fear, fear of exposure, fear of the truth, fear that all hell could break loose at any moment, grips their very being. They rush headlong to pass more laws like it would save their sorry asses when the shit hits the fan. Our government has forgotten that the people are the energy that drives the political vehicle in which they ride. We are the people that own the buildings where they do their business. We the people make it possible for them to parade through the halls and display the grandiose art work on the walls of the great structures they inhabit. They refer to them as federal buildings but it's the peoples' tax money that pays for those buildings. And when they assume that the people are their subjects, their beasts of burden, then it is time for them to hand over the keys because they are no longer sober enough to drive. We the people, is such a powerful statement that it goes over the heads of most people, or you have heard it so many times that it has lost its meaning. But let me remind you that this is your country. This country is not owned by the politicians. The politicians are HIRED HELP, PERIOD, and only hold a temporary position at best. They need to be reminded of that often. Law enforcement instructs its officers to never hand over your gun. Hostage negotiators never allow ransom to be a part of the deal. So learn a simple lesson from this. You don't have to negotiate with your hired help or your enemies. You instruct them to do the job or you will have no alternative but to let them go. This rule is simple and to the point. This government has so boldly intruded into your life via social security numbers, credit information, and now, thanks to George W. Bush and the passage of the Patriot Act, unauthorized wire taps and surveillance unlimited. But fear not my friends, we can surveil and expose them to the world via a variety of means. We can alert the world instantly. We can mobilize world wide in minutes. We can do the same as what recently happened in Iran with the riots in the streets over the crooked and stolen elections. We don't need a fifty thousand dollar camera and crew to capture the images and activity of these rodents to make news. The general feeling from the people is our government is rotten to the core. That is something that everybody already knows, and as is all governments, they are all imbued with this dictator mentality piously looking down on you as an unwanted guest at their party of enlightened assholes! We can follow their every move and document it and expose it to the world in an instant. Thanks to Al Gore's internet - tsk tsk. In Dick Morris and Eileen McGann's latest book "Catastrophe", you will find numerous predictions as to our government's activity. Our politicians have gotten away with their crocodile tears and apologies for their wrong doing for so long it has become an accepted bad habit and an expectation for the American people to just look the other way. Comments like, "It was just a moral misfire. It could happen to anyone", etc. They are mere human beings and nothing more, people. And a lot of bad ones at that!

Senator John Ensign of Nevada now admits to an affair with one of his political support ffteam mates and his close friend's wife, might

I add. It's June 2009, and here we go with South Carolina's Governor, Mark Sanford, just as I predicted in the few previous lines, crying those crocodile tears and begging forgiveness from his friends and family. What an idiot! What a scumbag idiot loser he is – and South Carolina's Governor! Walking the Appalachian Trail, deep in thought about how to best serve the citizens of the great state of South Carolina was grandiose bullshit. And on Father's

Day, he bounces out of the country to go visit his mistress and most likely on your dime. Sanford, Bill Clinton, John Ensign, George W. - they're all cut from the same pattern. They're all of the same moral fiber.   They do not concern themselves with anything but satisfying their lust for more and more. Who cares who it hurts, who cares? Let's look at what California is doing, now that they have had an out of control spending spree by those who were supposed to budget the peoples' money, those who are elected to be responsible to the people - good stewards of the peoples' government. Waste is all they have been able to accomplish - waste to the point that they have to send out IOU's to the people to whom they owe money. No big deal, just a nice little note and the price of a stamp, and I'll bet we all could get the IRS to defer our taxes permanently like some of their cronies at Goldman Sachs. You think maybe? Now California has passed a bill that legalizes selling marijuana, as long as the government controls it. I can remember a time back in the 1960's, when you would get jail time, lose your right to vote, and become pursued by the IRS for a few ounces of marijuana. But wait! There's more!! This is different. California needs the money to make up for the shortfall they are experiencing in revenue collection. You mean for over spending don't you? So, let me see if I can get this straight. The government of the state of California is pushing drugs to make M O N E Y? Isn't that against the law? Is that what you're saying? Copy cats, aren't they? This government body is like all government bodies not capable of running government, and because we the people do not kick the ass of these losers, we do not appoint the right people to office period. What we do is appoint people to office that can raise the most money. Government will change the rule book in an instant if they need anything or can't steal it from you. Like the days of prohibition. Now the government controls all liquors and alcoholic beverages. They will subsidize tobacco growers so they can collect tax from the end result. It is proven, you know, PROVEN - that tobacco causes multiple diseases and millions of deaths every year, but that doesn't mean anything to any form of government anywhere because they will, as an end result, play the odds whereby they will ultimately end up owning and running the health care system, and will treat you as they see fit - which keeps you in the loop but under their control. They want the money! The money! Look, you have to get hold of this one thing, this one fact - government talks out of both sides of its mouth. And any lie will do as long as they accomplish their goals. I remember a case in Nashville, Tennessee when an arena was being constructed within 500 feet of a church facility in the downtown area. First you must understand that there is a law that stipulates no establishment can be built within 500 feet of a church if that facility sells alcoholic beverages. In this case, the arena would sell alcoholic beverages, of course, because there would be entertainment performed at that facility, i.e. sports events, concerts, etc. Of course the Mama's and the Papa's of the local government got together in a pig fest and decided to change the law and allow the builders in question to continue with the church's blessing. NO MONEY EXCHANGED THERE, I BET. Now, do not ever allow this to come to the attention of a governing board when a private citizen wants to change the law to benefit private interest. When it is to benefit you and your interests all they can do is quote the law. There are still laws on the books in some states that you have to wonder what clown had convinced the passage of such lunacy. To find some of these laughable laws just do a search on the internet for them. Search for 'stupid laws or stupid law makers.

But now as we continue to focus on the problems we can do something about and what we must do in the face of what BO is attempting. You must realize your constitutional freedoms and your liberties will disappear if you do nothing about these slight of hand artists. Our congress doesn't have a spine, so anything goes. It looks like no one will oppose Obama. And if they do, they will only make it look like they are on your side. We will have one party calling the other on the carpet accusing them of whatever seems appropriate for the moment, attempting to engage the other side in outdated brainless word wars making it look like they are fighting on your behalf. This is only staging, showbiz, smoke and mirrors. There are those of you that will say I am too outspoken. But I will guarantee you there will come a time when you will change your mind. That time will come when you will be faced with the decision to crush your enemy or allow them crush you! I want you to get a copy of the book, "The Committee of 300" written by Dr. John Coleman, and published by World In Review. This is one of the most important pieces of literature you are likely to read in the present time. In fact, if you would like to know more about this author and discover a list of his works search and discover a treasure trove of information. It is my greatest hope that more people would start to investigate authority. Just because someone holds office in government or corporate, does not make them the ultimate authority. They only have a position and an opinion and nothing more. Do not give up your admiration and respect so easily to someone who is only on a different road or in a different position than you. Look for integrity and honesty in people – look for compassion, generosity. And look for a track record that proves without a doubt that the person who is asking for your vote and support has an agenda that fits with your core beliefs. I don't care if they are your local restaurant dishwasher or campaigning for the highest office in the land. You get the goods, and then base your decision on that, and still do so cautiously. The leadership in our government today is a sham and obviously controlled because no one could be that damned stupid and bold about it simultaneously. At the same time I hear radio and television commentaries blasting these mentally deficient hypocrites in our government, and yet they remain in office. I have often been tempted to call some of these self-appointed enlightened folks and ask them when the movement starts. When do we organize? When is the revolution? When do we roll Bubba? It seems that everybody is waiting on someone else to cast the first stone, make the first strike, fire the first shot, etc. Let me tell you - the first stone has already been cast! It has been cast by this insidious group of control freaks we call the government. It was cast years ago by those who control everything you do and your every thought. I'm sure we all think that we are our own person, but not so. We are a product of programming done by those in control of even our most high level individuals, our most powerful government officials and decision makers. We obey the laws of the land, and we conform daily to the new laws written by the law makers and sometimes, most of the time, we don't even know about them until we want to build something, open a business, buy a new car or even do some travel. We don't even know what the government has done to our food. Yet our health statistics show that cancer has developed in 1of 300 newborn males and in 1 of 333 newborn females. Downs Syndrome is present in 1 of 800. Seventeen percent of children have developed some form of disability. And, the level of Autism is at an all time high - this is alarming!! What ingredients are we as a nation consuming in our food? Could this be a marker to the disease and birth deformation in some children?

Furthermore, what are their tax plans if we earn x-amount of money? There are tax options on the table that you don't even know about. They make campaign promises that tickle your ears, and we fall all over ourselves lapping up the bullshit like thirsty unsuspecting animals on the way to slaughter. Departments of this government specifically monitor your emotions as you listen to campaign speeches that rise with emotion when certain words are used and certain sentences are spoken. Your applause is heard, and your responses enjoyed. So they know exactly how to design their lies. Barack Obama's about-face on his campaign promises has had devastating effects on his popularity poll ratings over the past few weeks, but we loved what he said during his campaign. And now he is your President for the next four years regardless of how low his poll numbers fall. He is also riding low with the people that donated money to his campaign and supported his agenda. You have been lied to, and you have been suckered into the oldest con game in American history!! You put your trust in a politician - BAD BET BABY, but don't feel bad. All you have to do to recover is use the same amount of energy to get him out of office that you put into getting him elected. But for most of you, that won't happen will it? Why? Because the excitement is gone and all the emotion has dissipated, and you are all alone in your confusion. What happened? All is not lost though, your mission now, however, is to give America back to its original owners - the American people! Americans have lost the greatest possession they ever owned, AMERICA itself. We're no longer free in this country, just as most people around the world are not free. Our Presidents are not free thinkers. They are told what to think and what to do and how to act. And when they step on toes, or step out of line, they are shown with swift and dramatic consequence by whom and what might be in control. Consider Kennedy and Nixon, and their demise. And now we all have Barack Obama. As Bill O'Reilly put it, we have a President who doesn't understand presidential power. And I'm telling you, he has an arrogant attitude and a 'do it my way or else' mind set. He is nothing more than a puppet waiting to hear from those who are handing down his orders! The only thing that will get his attention is a shocking taste of reality. It will take a philosophical ass whipping to make him, and those like him, fear returning to work period! All the radio talk show and television hosts who propagandize and promote conservative or liberal philosophy should be the ones charged with organizing a movement to give America back to its original owners. It is they who have voices across the air waves and can reach the masses faster than us lowly defenders of freedom. They get paid well, but it is we who will pay the price. We don't mind, in fact, we welcome the challenge and the opportunity. The masses are charged with enough pent up energy and frustration against those whom have attempted to steal our birthright, our freedoms, and to enslave us; and we have taken all we're going to take. The tea party was nothing, just a friendly notice to voice our dissatisfaction with the elected powers that be. The people in this country are growing discontented more every day with these morons that think they are in charge. I don't think, however, when this thing starts to unravel, that you will see father against son and sons and daughters against their own families. I do, however, believe there will be some families split because of career, police and law enforcement professionals in general. I don't think that you will see police against citizens for the long term. I believe that you will eventually see a merging of forces by and between police and citizens to destroy a rogue government hell bent on enslaving the masses with an attempt to impose a one world order and a one world government. Every attempt to take your firearms is laughable and only brings us closer to the showdown that is going to be the defining moment of what is ultimately inevitable. Of course, the snakes that want everything you have through forced government programs have labored long and hard for many years to get to where they are today. But now is the time for opposition to move on what the BO administration is attempting to do with our health care system, our financial freedom and our individual rights. I am so disappointed in what this man has done with the position he holds. He has insulted your and my intelligence with his arrogant and deceptive promises. He is looking more and more every day like an egotistical fool with a punk mentality, and a rebel without a clue. Answering the public's health care questions with shallow sarcasm while in a public televised forum is about as presidential as a common con man. What a disappointment that must be to the people who gave this phony the millions of dollars in campaign contributions. I have more respect for the common crook. At least you know with whom you are dealing and what you can expect.

Our government is dangerously in debt to China, yes, communist China, and they want you and me to trust them with running our health care system? Our government has wasted this country's industrial industry and is surgically removing the muscle from our nation's financial and military standing. Our automobile and insurance industry is under attack. These losers can't find their asses with both hands and a road map, and yet, they want you to trust them to run this country's health care system? When it comes to rescuing the American people from their slowly disappearing constitutional rights by this government, they don't recognize us as U.S. citizens. They are not representing us. They are our ENEMY. They are attempting to bring America to its knees! They are hell bent on taking your guns from you so they will have no opposition. Step back and look at America from the perspective as a non-citizen. Can you look at America as it was fifty years ago, a hundred years ago, proud and strong? Everyone was pulling together. People are standing in line to become citizens of the greatest country in the world. This country was a shining example of freedom, the land of opportunity with deep respect for your government. We are a country with a peoples' bill of rights and a constitution that put everything in perspective. This is where both sides, the citizens and government, knew where the other stood, and they respected that. You were proud to support your government, a government proud of its citizens. Where are we today? We have little to be proud of in terms of government. We have even less to be proud of in terms of a President. We have recognized that we have a land filled with illegal aliens and a government that passes off the concern of its citizens with some flippant response to be tolerant. We have a President that calls a law enforcement officer 'stupid' without having any evidence to do so - only that the officer was a white man and the accuser was a black man. That is radical racism by this country's Commander and Chief. This is something that we have fought long and hard to eradicate. Racism is something that that has no place in our leadership period! Jumping to conclusions is not one of our President's strong suits nor does it show a great level of intelligence. It is very dangerous to have the person in the position of this country's ultimate power make this kind of rush to judgment and have such a lack of self control of one's emotions. Whatever he does from this point is almost expected to be out of line with the will of the American people. As one would expect, now the President of the United States is creating more and more division between the people of this country and himself. While on tour of the Asian regions of the world, he stands on foreign soil and announces that he will bring the accused terrorists that attacked America on 9/11 to be tried in the American court system. I can tell you that this is going to cause some backlash to his administration that will not go away soon, or if ever. I would think seriously that this should have been announced in America to Americans first. He will not be forgiven for this kind of insult to the American people. I, as well as many Americans, believe this should have been treated as a military matter since it was an act of war against this country. We as a country are still at war all these years later at a cost of so much more than anticipated by our educated idiots in Washington, and now we're going to give the accused terrorists access to our constitution, and our courts. HOW BRILLIANT! There are opposing views obviously from both parties and a division by and between the people of this country regarding this decision. Just look around you at the confusion that is caused by not only the federal government, but by local governments as well.

As of 2009, take a look at California's financial dilemma and tell me to be tolerant. Who is going to pay for this mess? It isn't something that is just going to go away on its own.   The situation must be addressed - something obviously our governments are incapable of.   There is more to this than the regular 'just wait and see' crap. We don't have to wait and see - we know. We the American people, fucking know! This is not just about debt that the American people will ultimately be stuck with. This also includes health and safety issues. This includes security issues. I know, I know, we have touched on this before. But we are reflecting on the greatness of this country as it was then, and as it is now. We are looking at how much this country has fallen behind because of a lack of responsible leadership. We have fought communistic doctrine and philosophy tooth and nail. We have rescued people from oppressive communistic leadership and dictatorship for as long as I can remember. And now we are doing business with them in the form of borrowing money from foreign countries in the hundreds of billions and trillions of dollars! We have an irresponsible leadership that is spending like a drunken sailor! There is no one at the helm and we are approaching a most turbulent storm!!!   This government has a lot of explaining to do to the American people. I don't intend to stand by and be silent as we sink from being so overloaded with the financial irresponsibility and of the leadership such as we have in this country. It is your and my responsibility to grab these drunken sailor types and slap the crap out of them until they sober up. We have not only the responsibility, but the right and the obligation to do so. Comedian and Actor Robin Williams' take on politicians is that they are like diapers and need to be changed often, and for the same reason, as he states in the film "Man of the Year". Yes, we must have a government. But we again, must have one that serves the will of the people, as I continue to hammer on. We all know what we have presently is not that government. Unless we act now and keep on acting in a positive and definitive manner, this country will slip into what the enemies of America have had in mind for a long time - a country so immobilized because of its loss of moral and ethical direction and its liberal obesity that it can hardly open its eyes to recognize its own emergency!! Look at what is going on all around us. We have fifteen million Americans out of work, yet the American government brings 1.5 million foreign workers each year into the U.S. We have traitors working against us; elected officials employed by our own government. Yet we are paying their salaries with our tax money. YOU AND I ARE PAYING SOMEONE TO DEFEAT US THROUGH THE DECISIONS OF OUR OWN GOVERNMENT OFFICIALS! I hope that you are grasping what I am telling you. Read this book twice if you must, and then call a friend and have a discussion of your own regarding what is happening in our country. Make notes and compile information. Get your neighborhood involved and have appointed leaders conduct research on specific topics. Start a publishing company and self-publish through the internet, if there is an internet left to communicate with. Let the world know what is happening in this country. I'll bet you that you will discover that people in foreign countries are experiencing the same thing. The leaders of the world governments are all in it up to their eyeballs. But don't take my word for it. See what comes back in the form of response to the information you expose through your writings, etc. I speak to people from all over the world and they all, I said ALL, have the same disgust for their government as I do for some in this government. The U.S. government is growing more obese every day, imposing their will more and more, yet we have failed to respond in like manner until now with the town hall meetings.

The rush to push this health care plan through when not everyone has completely read or understands it is too suspicious. It is not scheduled to go into effect until 2013, which is also suspicious and needs to be looked at with extreme scrutiny, especially when you are going to be taxed on it as soon as it passes, if it does - WHICH IT WON'T. I knew that the frustration of the American people with their government had reached a boiling point, and I had hoped that the town hall meetings would be publicized more fairly, but as governments are famous for, they have resulted in shifting the blame onto the American people. And now they are calling the American people un-patriotic because of the opposition to what we perceive as socialized medicine and more government control, both of which I totally agree. What the government in one sense of the matter is attempting to do is push a bill that serves government while it limits care and controls the peoples' needs at government's discretion. This bill is obviously loaded with objectionable un-digestible hidden government deception that the people are just not going to take. I don't have the information at this point that allows me to project any facts beyond what I have already stated, but I will return to this section as soon as I do. Senator

Pat Leahy, Democrat of Vermont, however, sees clearly enough it seems. He has established and developed a website, www.bushtruthcommission, and is calling for action from the American people to sign up and open investigations regarding the Bush/Cheney administration's alleged wrong-doings and will possibly take action to bring charges against them for their abuse of powers. Maybe he's just doing this to make himself look good and secure his position as senator for another term or two. He is a politician you know, but let's hope he gets the goods. I'll even pay for the rope!! But I will never support anyone that uses these underhanded tactics as politicians often do. You hear them all the time use their phony jargon to make it sound like they are so respectful of their fellow politicians. Remember, it is often said when a politician pats you on the back for a job well done they're just looking for a place to stick the knife. They all scream that the government is too big to be functional. Yes, they say this when you're watching and listening, but behind your back they have tons of additional overwhelmingly expensive programs that are readied for passage into law. Again most of their proposals have never even been read by anyone other than those who wrote them. They're just political favors. They tell each other "sign this for me, and I'll sign yours when you need it". There are bills that don't require congress to pass them into law. The finance committee can, with the stroke of a pen, pass laws you have never heard of or proposed bills about which you have forgotten. You must remember that they expect the public to continue to do what they have always done with their short term memory - forget what happened six months ago, a year ago, five years ago, etc. Remember they are constantly planning legislation. That's what they do; they pass laws that involve government in every aspect of your lives. From the amount of air that goes in your tires, to the amount of sugar that goes in your ketchup, to what your children are taught in school. And, they have also hidden the fact from you that you are sending your children to government run schools to learn government taught programs. Teaching only what government wants your children to learn. Calling schools public schools instead of what they really are. They are really government schools. Public transportation is really government transportation. Public parks are really government parks. Insignificant you might say, until you think what no child left behind really is. Now, everybody gets a passing grade. No one fails school, everyone is given a diploma whether they earned it or not. Now you have a society that you have to realize is ill qualified to do anything but just keep their heads down and never question anything, especially government. You have a society that they can control because they have brainwashed the citizens into becoming dependent on government, and that's just what government's intention is all about. Is it any wonder why there are so many gangs? The answer is simple. Maybe the gang members can't explain it yet because they haven't figured it out yet. This government would rather have you become a dumb ass than someone who is educated and can figure out that your intelligence is POWER. Just having a job is something that's going to always have you struggling. Most intelligence peddlers call having a JOB, 'Just Over Broke'. If you're just over broke, you will never reach your full potential because you will always be the slave to your 'just over broke' job, for 'just over broke' money. You will always be working for money instead of having money work for you. Without an education, life will control you. You will never control your life. Although many opportunities may come your way, you know you can't take advantage of them because you just don't qualify, you don't have the expertise, and you don't have the education. But you know that deep inside, you want to be in charge. You want to be in control of your life and your destiny. Well there is always a gang some where who wants someone like you because you are angry, you are hungry for recognition, you are intense. You are one mean ass bro, and this has been growing in you since you got out of school with that, no child left behind undeserved bullshit diploma. You'll show them who the hell you are won't you? Then there goes another life down the toilet. And this time it's yours! Your life was nothing more than a disappearing puff of smoke. Eunice Kennedy Shriver, who recently passed away in August 2009, at the age of 88, founded the Special Olympics. She was the sister of the Kennedy brothers, Bobby, Ted and John F., was raised in a family wherein their father demanded their upbringing be positive and focused. He taught them 'whatever you do, whatever you attempt, you don't fail and you don't come in second place. You are a Kennedy, You win!' That's the mentality you must have. You are an American. You must realize your life is WORTH SOMETHING. Your life is the only one you have. Are you going to let someone take it from you in the form of a hypocrite like what we have in our government? Leave a legacy that the world will revere your efforts and contributions to humanity. A gang will not do that for you!! Do something spectacular if you are a gang member!! Change your gang, your whole gang; take a stance. Be an example. You be a model for change to everyone in your gang. Rise above what everyone knows about you and become a winner. You want to fight someone? You want to kick some ass? Start looking at America's biggest problem makers. Start investigating the scum at the top. There is a starting point. And if you still don't get it, start helping a child that's deprived or one that has the propensity to lean toward where you just came from. Children are vulnerable and confused at a certain age, especially in their teenage years. They are fragile and uncertain just like you once were. Deep inside their minds they know that it's wrong to just kill something. But we have idiots that pass laws that say its okay to abort an innocent unborn at someone's request because you tell them you can't afford to raise a child or you will be uncomfortable in your bathing suit, or it's a woman's right? Where are your priorities? Sit down and look at what's important. You must question people in positions of power. Where with the stroke of a pen they start illegal wars that cost the lives of countless innocent people and waste billions of dollars that could be used to eradicate disease or feed the hungry and educate the illiterate. They condemn the innocent through the act of abortion because they fail to possess any common sense, any moral sense - any sense at all. Don't rule on the law if you don't know the law. Pass the baton over to someone who has at least one brain cell for Christ's sake! Is your ego and phony selfish pride so intense that you had rather kill an innocent unborn so you won't look stupid in front of the other stupid ones in your league? Or, is it that neither you nor anyone else has the integrity or can make an informed decision? So now the teenager grows up with the idea that it's okay to kill because he learned this in his formative years, so he goes to school and one day just decides to waste a group of his classmates because he doesn't like the way they handle themselves in the gym class or in the lunch room. Well you can thank Roe v. Wade and those that passed abortion it into law.

Don't condemn the teenager. We are the ones to blame because we didn't riot in the streets and drag those scumbags that passed those laws down to the river and give them one last chance to reverse the law before we fit them to a pair of concrete shoes. I'll bet you anything that things would have been a lot different if you had done something about it. Now you have women saying they have the right to have abortions like it's no different than deciding whether or not to have a bag of popcorn at the theatre. The cat is out of the bag brother, and it's going take some time to stop this run away immorality! I'm not speaking from a religious point of view but from a common sense point of view. Ever since the Supreme Court, the ACLU and Madalyn Murray O'Hair and Rowe v. Wade arrived on the scene prayer left the schools, the Ten Commandments were removed from the court houses and public view, and abortion laws were left in place as law. Do you expect anything less from a child that has been educated in a government school? How do you reprimand a child that follows your example and is able to quote you the law? How do you expect a child to learn that it's okay to kill the innocent unborn that has done nothing to deserve the death sentence in such a cruel way, and not the bully that steals your lunch money everyday or the gang that rapes his sister? How do you expect a child to act any differently when all the indicators point to the fact that's its okay for the rest of the world to kill at will, but not for him or her, the ones who have been humiliated and victimized by a gang of bullies on the school yard. That's just one of the rationales that must go through a confused kid's mind. We as Americans have allowed these swollen heads in Washington to pass laws that are in direct opposition to what we hold as morally correct. We know the ramifications of wrong decisions because we have been the ones who suffer the loss of our children in some senseless school shooting disaster or gang related murder or illegal war. So now we have those same swollen heads try to convince us that it's the gun laws, and that all guns need to be confiscated, and that the constitution should be amended to make all guns illegal. Not so fast bubba. What has to happen here is we must turn this government upside down and shake all the immoral sense out of these demonic lovers of deception. Now I'm going to say that if the laws presented or up for review are not reviewed by at least a panel of people with more than one brain cell between them, then wait for a higher power to intervene. What I am saying is that the American people are smarter than a whole host of most so called supreme justices. Common sense and moral content is something everybody could carry around in their pocket for awhile. I don't mean religious content; religious content could be anything. I don't need to elaborate. But the laws that do however get enacted and eventually become law, must not in any form encroach on, or tread on anyone's religious rights period. It is harder to get laws or people recalled or ousted from office than it is to get laws passed to kill the innocent and start illegal wars. Consider pervert Congressman Mark Foley and Congressman William Jefferson, both caught with the goods. And as expected, pervert Mark Foley wants to pass the blame off on some pervert priest in his past, but the evidence was so overwhelming that there was no chance of any other means of escape. Congressman William Jefferson tried to lie low and fly beneath the radar, but it just wasn't meant to be. He was just convicted and sentenced to 13 years as of November 2009. The evidence was so overwhelming that on August 5, 2009, a federal jury convicted the now former congressman on 11 of 16 counts, one from when agents found

$90,000 cash in his freezer. He was accused of accepting more than $400,000 in bribes and seeking millions more for brokering deals outside the U.S. Jefferson could have faced 180 years if he had been convicted on all charges. Travers Mackel, of NBC station WDSU of New Orleans and the Associated Press, was the source of this report. The young people all over the world are ready to carry out a meaningful charge on corruption, but for the most part are uninformed. While on the other hand the older citizens, who are more informed, tend to analyze to the point of inaction. Well that's okay; the old took care of the young when they could not take care of themselves and now it's time for the young to take care of the old who cannot muster the strength to lead the charge against corruption, but who are more than willing to support and educate the young in their battle and opposition in this ever present danger now in our government. As author Michelle Malkin states in her book "Culture of Corruption", "We cannot allow this country to create illegal wars and use those wars as an excuse to take more and more rights from the citizens of this country by saying the constitution is overridden here because we are at war and then use that kind of excuse to attempt passage of more patriot acts." Most of the citizens of this country do not realize the dirty underhanded maneuvers to which this government will reach to control you and eliminate any rights you may have. You don't realize just how close you are to becoming victimized, just as the citizens of Iran have recently been victimized in attempting to establish a legitimate government, as you will see next.

It is August 2009, and Iran has put to death over a hundred of the rioters that charged the government with stealing the election. Some were so brutally beaten while in jail that they never made it out alive. They were Iran's youth, so willing to sacrifice their lives for a non-corrupt government. Countless others will face the challenge in the months to come. They are willing to die to get this kind of garbage out of government and get the proper representation in place. Not like here in the good old USA. We are all over the place. We on one hand condemn child molesters that operate in the shadows of the back alleys and the streets, but allow them to operate openly in Catholic churches. You see, we are horrified when we see a child get shot in school, but abortion is legal. It is illegal to raise marijuana in your back yard, but the state of California has set up shop in the city where you can come by and pick up some because you're feeling out of sorts. There is something to be said when people all over the world are dissatisfied with these governments operating under a double standard. The government that does not serve the people will surely be dealt with. Common logic tells me that governments, all governments, had better reassess their position on human rights. Human rights are not given by governments, and they will not be taken away by governments no matter how many must die fighting for that right. As I have stated many times, and as I will continue to say, there must be something wrong when the entire world is opposed to what their governments have become. Some societies are just awakening while others are already in battle. The one good thing is that the internet is a fabulous tool whose time has come. It allows other countries to peer into what might seem at times, a strange reality. The other day I was talking to someone from outside the U.S. and they asked me where they might find a restaurant that served pancakes or waffles. I, of course, directed them and they told me they never had the luxury of having such wonderful foods except maybe once or twice a year on very special occasions. If they think that waffles and pancakes with butter and syrup are good, just watch what happens when the rest of that world gets a taste of freedom. That is why, at all cost, we must protect our freedoms and our God-given rights from those who would steal or restrict our way of life and especially when so many have fought and died for that cause so others who want nothing more than the opportunity to work and raise their families in peace and live in freedom. What comes from the greedy controlling minds is that they hate to see people free to choose, that hate to see people succeed, they hate to see anyone but themselves reach the top. This is the miserable dark mind that likes to get theirs by having you lose yours. This is insanity. Satan, according to certain religious beliefs, has the ability to appear as an angel of light in order to deceive. So be careful whom you trust, especially those whom have succeeded in completing the climb to the pinnacle of the political ladder. They have a goal in mind, and you might have contributed to their success. Never trust man or demon for they are one in the same if the opportunity is right.

You see Kim Jung Il of North Korea, the little dictator monkey, ordering brandy by the hundreds of thousands of dollars for himself and his cronies, while some of the people of North Korea struggle daily for food just to survive. Struggling for food on a daily basis for their children is a reality. Go to Cuba and other dictator-ruled countries and try to buy a brand of food or brand of medicine other than the state brand. You won't find it anywhere because it doesn't exist there. You will buy what the state tells you to buy. There is only one brand and that's the state's brand. Now that Fidel Castro is reaching the end of his life, there are people celebrating his death and chanting to rush his departure, celebrating in the streets the end of this tyrant and his stranglehold on the Cuban people. Finally, there is the feeling of freedom from this thug. While Cuba is absolutely physically beautiful, it has been an ugly place to be because of Castro. Maybe when he is worm bait and the Cuban people have the freedom to choose, and there is finally once again free enterprise, Cuba will bloom to its full potential. Before Fidel Castro took over, Cuba was a fine place for tourists to visit and vacation. Don't we ever see clearly the pattern forming as it is brought to our attention? Governments have always treated people with some form of disrespect, and ruled them like cattle in many instances. But now the sun is setting on the old rule and a new revolutionary mindset is evolving. The world is watching Sudan murder its own people through starvation and genocide. These tyrants need and deserve to be eliminated in the same way they are killing their own citizens. They need to be starved until their rotten asses beg to be shot. But make sure when they expire, that they are left on top of the ground so the flesh eating foul and the carnivorous beasts devour and dispense of their rotten carcass. They will not escape the wrath and the literal hell that they so lavishly bestowed upon their own people. That my friends, is a picture of some governments out of control, and that my friends, is a snapshot of the future of America. I see it, I feel it, and I know it. Some may say that is a rash statement, but let's start looking at how government creeps and spreads its heinous cancerous agenda so slowly that it is hardly even noticed by the people.

As a means of American government control, currently there is a RFID tracking chip imbedded in all passports issued to those leaving this country, America, on vacation or business travel. And that RFID chip has all of your personal information in it. Of the 2,335 comments received on the RFID plan, 98.5% were negative, but the Bush administration chose to go ahead with the plan of embedding the 64kb chips in all future passports, citing a desire to abide by globally interoperable standards devised by the International Civil Aviation Organization, a United Nations agency. So that should tell you that no matter how overwhelmingly opposed to something you may be, if the government wants to impose whatever their plans are on the citizens of this country, which seems to be the case with the health care bill, they will do so unless you cause fire from hell to fall on their heads. This is in all reality your only option.

Sixty-eight percent of the people of the U.S. don't want the health care bill in its present state. That is a majority. That gives the government 32%. This is dangerous, and Obama is more dangerous. He is like a deadly poisonous snake loose in your room with the lights out. We now look at our government as an extravagant ugliness that spreads and promotes policy known for its deception by not only its own citizens but now by how the rest of the world also looks at America. In the eyes of the rest of the world, we are a dangerous aggressor nation. Just after the attack on Iraq, and the discovery was made that there were no weapons of mass destruction, I had the opportunity to speak with someone from Canada regarding their massive sand oil fields. I told them that I was amazed when I discovered the size of their oil fields were larger than that of Saudi Arabia. They responded jokingly, "please don't attack us". All of us laughed it off as harmless humor as we continued with respectful niceties and general conversation throughout the rest of the day. I couldn't forget that lodged in the minds of all of us was the fact that there was the thought and possibility that nations could turn on each other whether they were neighboring border nations or countries somewhere across the globe and that we sometimes have to apologize for the leadership and representation we have in our own countries. I hate to even recognize the fact that we have those like John Kerry who blatantly insults our troops serving on active duty in our military. Kerry is a brainless elitist who on CNN, stated that you must get an education, do your homework or end up in Iraq.

Glenn Beck's response was classic. I thought he would have a heart attack. But we do however in this country, tolerate this stinking garbage like Kerry. It's just a shame that he gets paid to embarrass everyone with his brainless statements. If you watched CNN's "Broken Government", you have to know that the current congressmen and women are criminals and they are escaping prosecution and shoving it right up your nose, America's nose, and no one is doing anything about it. However, a few do get caught like Tom DeLay, William Jefferson, Clinton, and the likes. But how stupid do you have to be to call attention to yourself? We as people all have a built in tolerance of support and resistance, like a beam of steel, has a built-in tolerance of support and resistance. However, unlike steel, we uniquely have what is known as emotion. And that emotional stress level is presently at its maximum. We watch congress go to work a couple days a week to seemingly represent everyone but the Americans, grab their pay checks, grab a little bit more from the lobbyist and then they have someone take them for a free lunch, a round of golf, and then it's off for a little adulterous activity and a cocktail. But watch what happens to those who would consider themselves above the law. Let's go back a few years to the time when Iraq leader Saddam Hussein was found guilty and sentenced to hang along with the rest of his untouchables. That occurred even though the war with Iraq was and is illegal, just to state an 'in your face' reality comparison.

Somehow, someway reality will present itself when you least expect it, and you will be snared like a rabbit - fallen from your lofty perch to go down in our history as the traitors you are. Your photos or images, however, may appear in our history books, but they will never appear on our money unless it happens to be like you - counterfeit. That is what you are, and that is what you are all about, how fitting. Remember this, the powerful do what they have the power to do, while the weak accept what they must accept. The elitist politicians will ultimately remember one thing if they learn nothing else ever. The governed will only be governed to a point. This book is being written and compiled during the latter part of the Bush Administration and the beginning stages of Barack Obama's rise to power, and I am watching the transition and transformation as it unfolds daily. BO is promising some of the same shit that Bush promised. But I will predict that he will deceive the nation as did Bush. BO at least has the ability to string two words together, and that will work well for him temporarily. However, I think he will come very close to transforming this nation in a very dangerous and negative way. I have said and will continue to say, the government's first obligation and responsibility is to the people of this country and to their welfare and safety. And though I believe that this is a very dangerous time to attempt to lead any nation, I do, however, admire anyone who has the proper and clear focus to improve and strengthen a country when turbulence and turmoil is everywhere. People are fed up though with the kind of leadership we have experienced in the past, and the people will make it tough for anyone who is asking for their trust and support, whether they agree with the candidate or not. We all know there would be no wars if it weren't for politicians, dictators, rulers, and greedy international bankers. This country is sickened by the fact that their family members pay with their lives for someone's personal vendetta, right Bush? Still this government wants the people to put trust in government to develop a government health care system. Yeah, right - and at a time when half of the uninsured are here illegally. That's one reason you won't get my vote. This government wants you and me to pay for their coverage up front as well and wait a few years before your coverage kicks in. I'm tired of being insulted aren't you? That's the second reason you won't get my vote. You want America's support in getting the health care billed passed, and as of this writing none of you has read this bill. That's the third reason you won't get it. We don't want your sugar-coated crap!!! Garbage is garbage, I don't care how much honey you pour over it. This country's citizens should be covered with the best health care money can buy without ever kicking in another single cent, simply because of the tax monies already stolen and wasted by this government in the hundreds of trillions of dollars. Instead, this government wants taxation that supports more and more government waste, more government bailouts that go for executive bonuses. That's the fourth reason you won't get my vote. No public option in the health care bill is the fifth reason you won't get it. And now watching you flip-flop and squirm because you have nothing to offer the people of this country, only shows me you had nothing to offer the first time around. All this administration wants to do was make itself look good and sound good while slipping the old wiener to the American people once again, giving government total control of the health care system. Friends, if that ever happens you will never get it back. You must realize that once government gets its grubby little fingers on anything to control, you lose. LISTEN CLOSELY... GOVERNMENT CANNOT IMPOSE A NATIONAL HEALTH CARE SYSTEM ON YOU BY FORCEING YOU TO PURCHASE THEIR HEALTH CARE POLICY. When and if this attempt by government should happen, then you, as a citizen have the perfect opportunity and the right to revolt. Because at that time, there will already be a full blown revolution in place. And at that time, you will be living under communist rule. Forcing you to buy government policy is communistic. Our constitution forbids that – period! Obama is simply continuing what Bush started, so lay the blame where you. Until this government starts to represent the American people, they will get nothing from the American people! We are living in a most awesome and exciting time. Look, we have a most powerful military, in all branches. We have capability that most people or countries haven't the imagination to conceive, and yet we elect people that are incapable of such awesome responsibility, people that become over zealous bullies; people that feel they can just push people and countries around because they are in possession of such power and capability. This country cannot gamble with such as that. Look to the past. Look at Pearl Harbor, the wars with Germany, Vietnam and Iraq. These were all designed wars. Think not; do a little research before you start to criticize that statement. Those conflicts have devastated everyone but politicians, international bankers and the manufacturers of weapons. And we the taxpayer, pay for every stinking dime of it. Oh, we the taxpayers are a useful commodity aren't we? To destroy our enemies would require that we investigate ourselves, meaning our own leadership, our own government. Greed and power is and has always been at the center of the problem that every society faces. Unless you control power, it will control you. Unless you control money, it will control you. Unless you control the leaders they will control you. Look at Darfur – 400,000 innocent lives wasted (as of the writing of this book.) Something is wrong when a government murders its own people by whatever means it chooses, whether mowing them down with machine guns or starving them to death, there is no difference. Bottom line is that innocent people loose their lives at the hands of murderers in their own governments. Clearly, when a government uses this kind of aggression against its own people, this awesome power is in the wrong hands. When a president can go to war on a whim and connected governmental departments fail or refuse to use the legal checks, balances and restraints, be it dictator, king, ruler or president, those leaders need to be brought under control. Those governments deserve no second chances, and those leaders need to be removed from all power immediately. Those governments are guilty of genocide. So, if you are a president and you create a war and disguise it to look like something else, like a terrorist attack or threat of weapons of mass destruction, what do we do then? Let them go? Let them slither off into the underbrush like the snakes they are? I don't think so. But the rest of the world stands by and does nothing while all these helpless people are slain - proving once again, over and over that the lives of innocent people mean nothing. This is a government that the world community must hold guilty. But we wait like we did until Hitler finished murdering six million Jews.

Then we write our little stories and produce our little news programs while the atrocities break out somewhere else in the world. It seems that there is more condemnation towards the comedian Michael Richards for using the word nigger in an attempt to be funny with his comedy set than there is for the 400,000 murder victims of Darfur and the innocent victims of the Iraq war, including civilians and military alike. It is easier for the politically correct to condemn a comedian for the wrong choice of words than it is for all of us to come together and demand that the international community do something about the outright genocide taking place in those countries, as well as bring charges against our own leadership for such atrocities, when and if necessary. There, my friends, is sufficient evidence and legitimate reason enough for the prosecution of any and all, if necessary, of the United Nations leaders. The decider Bush pushed this government to go to war with Iraq for personal and political, as well as business reasons. And the congress let him get away with it by doing nothing which makes them accessories to the same crimes by their inaction alone - just as guilty as Bush and Cheney. Comedian Richards made a stupid mistake, but that is nothing compared to the mistakes we in this population are making by doing nothing to rescue those innocent and helpless people from the heavy hand of oppressive government. We as a body of nations need to commit to overthrowing those kinds of governments in the name of humanitarian principles. The United Nations won't do it. They are too busy feeling important and admiring their grandiose reflection on the world stage. They let the poisonous venom from the minds of these oppressors complete their dirty work and then act disturbed and surprised at such atrocities, but continue letting those respectful world statesmen and the likes of the Bushes slither away into the underbrush like the snakes they are, and yet failing to prosecute the entire bodies of government for failing to uphold the constitution of the United States is a crime that we the American people are committing. Simply by the office congress holds, bind them by oath to uphold the constitution. They have all broken that oath to the American people. That makes the office they hold, a fraud, period! Bush handed the baton off to BO to further diminish America on the world stage and further diminish the freedoms and rights guaranteed to all of us by this United States of

America's constitution and the people's bill of rights. Now that BO has secured a position for government in the financial markets, at your expense - the auto industry, at your expense - and soon what he hopes will be in the health care industry, at your expense, is only the beginning. He wants to have the power to control the internet in the event of an emergency. You had better fight this with all that you can muster. THIS MAN, BO, IS THE ULTIMATE ENEMY OF YOUR FREEDOMS! But in my personal opinion, he is nothing more than the latest turd in the political punch bowl. The American Center for Law and Justice (ACLJ) chief counsel, Jay Sekulow, is investigating BO's attempt to take control of the internet in case of an emergency as an unconstitutional maneuver. But with BO's appointed czars who seem to be circumventing the constitution and the laws and rights we have for so long enjoyed, we are in for a good fight. The polls regarding this latest maneuver of controlling the internet in the event of emergency has shown 100% of the people disapprove of the president having that kind of power and for good reason. We know what that would lead to. Once any form of disease like the one we have in our government infects our freedom further, we will never recover or regain full control of our losses without an absolute overthrow of our own government. You and I better gather our friends and families and join forces with the rest of the freedom loving Americans and defeat this administration's appetite for devouring our freedoms and our rights. The fairness doctrine is also under attack. The fairness doctrine, in this case means that if you have a conservative broadcast talk show, radio or television, you must also have a liberal talk show to balance the commentary. Even though the Supreme Court upholds that philosophy, the FCC has remained neutral in the sense that it does not believe that the FCC is responsible for enforcing the rule. This slowly creeping loss of your freedoms goes unnoticed for the most part because we are so busy working to keep life on track that we hardly notice the noose tightening. But when you are unable to breathe freely you will start to panic and then it will be too late. That day is fast approaching, and BO has his foot pressed to the metal. There are already giant billboards in place calling for Obama's impeachment because of his determination to destroy small business and the middle class. Remember, as the middle class goes, so goes the rest of society. Currently, the middle class is what is holding this country together. When the middle class disappears there will only be the rich and the poor classes left. Government knows that the rich do not want to lose their standing position and they also know the poor classes will do anything to rise to the top. Standing in the middle then will be the government controlling both the upper and the lower classes like puppets. The middle class is the only hope the lower class has in which to ascend because the middle is the next step up. A large legitimate American middle class is America's guarantee for success. It is the balance wheel that stabilizes this nation and every one of us, whether we know it or not, depends on it. Now is the time to start talking to your friends to find out what they know about our government's agenda. If you are a young person then its time to start communicating with your parents again - you'll be amazed at what they know. It's time to turn to your local AM talk radio or PBS radio stations. No, that is not un-cool. This is your country, too. This is your constitution, and this is your bill of rights. You have a voice, so USE IT. You want to belong to something larger than yourself, something over which you have some control? TAKE CHARGE OF IT. You'll be amazed to find out that maybe your strongest ally lives next door. Or, maybe that friendly person that always says hello, but always keeps to themselves is your worst enemy. This is not a time for violence, but a time for evaluating your friends. Don't argue political points with anybody. Just use care in choosing your ally's. Organize and form power groups because there is something sinister moving in the weeds and it is going to take all your strength and will to defeat it. This is the one time in your life that you cannot sit on the sidelines and expect anyone else to act on your behalf. Ignorance in this case, as the poets would have you believe, is not bliss. Ignorance, in this case, is dangerous and deadly. You have been the victim of a setup through our own government and the Federal Reserve System for years. You have been the slave to a system that has used you and threatened you and stolen from you for years, and continues to do so up to and including this very moment, and they are not about to let go just yet. You have been used by the Federal Reserve and the congress for years to support the losers at the top. There is nothing good, legitimate or legal about bailing out those who fail through lack of judgment or bad business practices. This government has been taking from the taxpayer and bailing out those in the banking industry any time one of the banks fail, every time a railroad line became insolvent, every time an auto manufacturer could not meet its financial obligations. And the beat goes on, and on, and on. You, the taxpayers have paid for every war we have ever had whether you knew it or not. You the taxpayer have paid for every weapon of war ever created, whether you knew it or not. You the taxpayer have paid to rebuild the very countries that our wars destroyed. What is or was the point? The point is, the international bankers that financed these created wars have become filthy rich on the heads and the backs of the innocent and the unsuspecting. It is this arrangement by and between the Federal Reserve, our government, and the international bankers who finance this murderous activity at your expense, sometimes hiding the real cost from you through inflation. Inflation - the unseen tax or what is often referred to as the hidden tax. Aside from the fact that you will never pay off the debt incurred by these war mongers, your children will live in debt for years as their standard of living decreases, which at present is declining at a rate of 30%. The losers and users at the top, who manipulate war, bank failure, business failure, forced taxation, and indebtedness all through illegal means, will watch their standard of living increase. However, you will once again be called upon for more tax increases while more of your sons, daughters, mothers and fathers will be called to fight in some other politically created war for oil or whatever flavor of the week happens to exist! The town hall meetings recently started in 2009, have awakened a slumbering spirit in some of our patriots in America. Families are enraged that BO is attempting to infiltrate the schools and persuade school children to follow his lead through what is perceived by many as socialist propaganda. What we must do now is continue to move with force and determination to push back the political enemies of America and the presidential appointed czars who seem to have no problem in attempting to destroy what has always held this country together, and that glue is the constitution and the bill of rights. We must never allow these timeless documents to be tread upon by the likes of the Clinton's, the Bush's, both H.W. and G.W., BO, the Nixon's, the IMF, the IRS, the Federal Reserve, the WTO, etc. I hate to think that this country is for sale, but it is. It sickens me to know that the upper echelon, the supposed representatives of the people have made deals with industry, both foreign and domestic, and countries that have agreed that governments will force the masses to pick up the tab for the failure of those who are at the top of the food chain through forced taxation. Governments make deals and pacts to hold down the wages of the masses while those on the other side of the coin continue to receive huge bonuses simply because they are politically connected. At present, we have in the United States over 3,500 lobbyists for a limited number of congressmen and senators. It is no wonder the ones who so humbly come to Washington who desire only to serve their country leave as multi-millionaires.

You think Bernie Madoff was a con artist? You think Enron was a rip off? Those and all like them are pip-squeaks compared to the underhanded thieves in our government and the Federal Reserve, which is, as a matter of fact and record, not Federal at all. Yet with the assistance of our congress, scumbags and traitors to the American people, like Senator Nelson Aldrich, one of the richest bankers of his time, were allowed to write the laws, while in conjunction with the congress to legitimize and legalize it all, to this day still govern America's currency. Those laws allow for the control, the printing, and the loaning back to America, of its own money at a rate of interest that keeps you, me, and all Americans perpetually financially enslaved. Wake up America!!! Everyone else is. In 2009, Japan, after fifty years of liberal government idiocy, is out on its ass, and a conservative government is in. The rest of the world also feels this push into doom by the kind of wasteful and irresponsible government that exists everywhere. It's time, right now to push back as hard as you can or you're going to drown. You're going to lose everything you have. Your currency is going to crash like a lead balloon, your health care is going to disappear and you're going to wake up to a socialistic government. Just like Thomas Jefferson predicted, you and your children, and your children's children are going to wake up homeless on the continent your forefathers fought and died for. I personally see this as a push for a one world currency because every country is in the deepest debt in which they have ever been, and it is frightening the hell out of most people. Our government is full of gangsters. Your schools are teaching homosexual and lesbian lifestyles as a normal way of life, and you're being told to just be tolerant. You are shamefully BUYING INTO IT! What the hell are you living for? This is a time to fight like you have never had to fight in your life. We have been asleep for a long time, but now it's time to wake up and face this unwelcome reality because as we speak, it is upon us. Do an internet search for www.ManhattanDeclaration.org. You will see what the Catholic organizations are doing to combat this outlaw government and its leadership. We have a repulsive pervert, Barney Frank, Congressman of Massachusetts representing the American people in the U.S. Congress. (BARF). We have Charlie Rangel, Chairman of the House Ways and Means Committee imposing tax law in everyone's lives while he lives an exempt life. Charlie Rangel wants to impose a military draft. Look, we would have no reason for a draft if these goobers in our government, yes that includes presidents with their writing statements, would not start the wars. It all leads right back to the top. The problems all start at the top and end at the top, ALWAYS. You can look throughout history, and the story is the same. It's always the same. The problems that we face today were started at the top yesterday. Dan Henninger calls this backlash of public dissatisfaction against the government, a revolt of the masses, and for good reason. We have a government within our government, gnawing and tearing at the fabric of the constitution, and leading the charge is none other than BO, the black oppressor himself. Corporations have moved off shore to other countries, away from our abusive tax system. And who is to blame but our own greedy self-serving unconstitutional government. They are the gang bangers and gangsters that are most dangerous. It is they who have the law on their side. THIS MUST CHANGE...THIS HAS TO CHANGE... THIS WILL CHANGE, AND IT IS YOU AND I WHO WILL BRING THE CHANGE. We have a President who has in fact, appointed at present time, about 30 czars, and these czars answer to no one but the President. That is not acceptable since it is we, YOU AND I, who pay their salaries. We have a president who, during his address, lies to the American people, and Congressman Joe Wilson of South Carolina calls President B.O. a liar in open forum, then apologizes. Well, wait just one minute. Who the hell got to him? In an instant he, Congressman Wilson, becomes my hero and in the next moment folds like a house of cards. We have a President who lies to us in his address and a Congressman who catches him in that lie and expresses his dissatisfaction on live television. Now look at this for what it is - the Congressman catches hell for voicing his dissatisfaction to a liar. The message here is what? You catch a liar, and call him a liar, and that is not acceptable because he is the President? What has he, the President, said he would do if he or his cabinet discovers any wrong doing by the congressmen or the senators? He, the President, said he would CALL YOU OUT... CALL YOU OUT!!! Enough said. Thank you, Congressman Joe Wilson, for calling out a liar. Being President does not erase the fact that President BO is in fact a liar. None of these dorks in Washington have anything more than a part-time job, and they certainly have no spine. But, if we don't keep our eye on them every waking moment, they can do great damage to this country. Czar Van Jones, who recently resigned, made some pretty far reaching statements, and a lot of them we know were racially charged. We know that race played a large role in getting BO elected, but I don't see the black community out in force wearing the tee shirts that read "WE DID IT" like we saw during the election. I think that for the most part the black society has a better view now of what the real agenda is from our newly elected LIAR President. Bush, Cheney, and Clinton were all liars, too. In fact, I don't know a politician that isn't a liar, so don't start with the racial bullshit with me. I'm not playing that game. I always call them like I see them, and I don't care what color you are, or what color you're not. We had better start looking at what character the politicians are instead of fighting amongst ourselves about what color someone is. In fact, that's just what the scumbags at the top want to happen. You have to realize, the way to win any battle, whatever the fight, is to overcome your opponent by dividing them and causing them to fight amongst themselves. That is what you must do at all cost. That is why we have a two party system. Get it? As I have stated many times, to win any battle, you must divide and conquer. That is one of the oldest battle strategies in the history of mankind. Get your enemies to start killing each other for you. Let them win the battle for you - outsmart them by allowing them to feel like the victor. We have let them confuse and frustrate us to the point that we lose to them through our own stupidity. Is that what you want? I don't think so. Greatness is not accomplished through what BO is attempting to do. Greatness is accomplished through becoming silent for a time, and standing still long enough to understand the direction of the wind. Greatness is accomplished by understanding the desire of the nation and the will of the people and helping them achieve it. Greatness is gaining support from the people you represent by having them represent you. Real power is the power of the people transferred to supporting you without having to ask, and not depriving the people of their rights and freedoms because you seek the power to control. This is the mark of a loser. The American people have awakened to the fact that they have been the cash cow for every nation on earth and every project government could dream up. The politicians have burdened the people with promises to other nations that the American taxpayer will bail them out if they start to fail in their efforts and obligations as developing nations or if they can't meet their obligations financially. I don't need that kind of egotistical, brain dead person representing me, do you? What has happened here is the politicians who are supposed to represent American interests have represented everyone but Americans. When borrowing nations have failed to be responsible to America in terms of their financial obligation and the monies just disappear, our government rushes in to renegotiate the loans and give more of your money with the understanding that this must happen in order for the banks to look like the developing countries have not defaulted on their loans. That my friends, is what has been happening for decades while hundreds of billions of your tax dollars have been used for others to live like kings. Yet hardly any of this money ever reaches its intended destination or gets used for its intended purpose. As we move along, you will discover more and more what has been happening to your money through the ever so generous politicians that are supposed to represent you. This needs to be exposed as do those who are responsible for such activity. Just like the sham in which the organization ACORN has been involved for years at your expense. If ACORN had not been exposed, they would have gotten away with a scheduled, $8 billion of taxpayers' money. They are the parasitic players that saw what stupid gullible representatives we have in our government representing the citizens, and they took advantage of it. Either that or they had an open door and a real strong connection to a power source higher up. But wait! Wasn't it BO that said, "ACORN will always have a permanent seat at my table"? They knew that the brainless, worthless parasites that represent the American peoples' interest barely have the energy to keep one eye open. Thinking or using their brain is entirely something else, far too extreme for what we have representing us. I actually believe that we have no one representing American interests or the American people in general. As a matter of fact, this kind of garbage has been going on for years, and no one has been doing anything to protect the peoples' interests. They just want you to keep pouring more and more of your money down the rat hole, because it shows the benefactor of your money that you will do anything your government tells you to do. I totally agree with Jerry Doyle, talk radio host. He says that we praise mediocrity. How absolutely right he is. That is exactly what we have as leadership in this country. 'Con artists and scum bags' are my choice of describing what we have in Congress, the Senate, and as President, BO doesn't have a clue. Yet he thinks he has got it all figured out. He is in my words, stupid, a liar, and an enemy of the people and this country, period. No apology. What a president has to do to accomplish an agenda, is satisfy the will of the people. The President is the peoples' servant in all reality. He/She is elected by the people to serve them, not to dictate to them. Find out what the people want and help them accomplish it. Toss your ego in the garbage and get to work along side the people and accomplish their wishes. This way everyone wins. Don't start dictating your agenda like you are the all knowing, all intelligent, upright walking slickest thing to come into view since the morning sun. I don't care how many educational degrees you have. A good old-fashioned sense of true direction is what people most appreciate and what they most respect in a president. This is the mark of a true leader. As Jerry Doyle once asked, "what great accomplishments have we made in the last fifty years?" I think we would have to ponder long and hard before we could answer, if we even have an answer. There doesn't seem to be a lot of great accomplishments. There seems to be a greater divide between government and the people than ever before. I understand it, but I think that a lot of people don't. I think that most people know something is wrong but don't want to point fingers without having the facts. I believe that the general population looks for answers from government, and I believe that is a big mistake. Those given the authority and awesome responsibility to make the critical decisions that guide this country properly seem to take that responsibility too lightly. This government's encroachment on our God-given rights infuriates me. As small as it may seem to some people, every move that government makes seems to somehow limit the citizens of their freedoms in some way. I truly believe that government needs to be controlled at every opportunity. Government is methodical and masterful at deception. Government doesn't want the people using the 'F' word, 'F' for Freedom. Government doesn't like us using the 'C' word, 'C' for Constitution. Government doesn't want us using the 'I' word, 'I' for Impeachment. Government doesn't want us using the 'R' word, for Revolution. Government has this disgusting deceptive ability to scheme its way around the true issues of importance and paint what is important and legitimate as just the opposite. But once passed into law, these broad strokes of pastels that looked good on the surface, will reveal the ugly beasts lurking in the shadows, which brings me back to the point of my mission in this world of removing these sleaze bags that seem to want nothing more than to enslave the citizens of this nation and to deprive us of our most basic rights. We need to waste no time in taking action and move swiftly against our government when this happens. Stop them in their tracks and tie their hands so they are not allowed to authorize another cent of bailout money to any other country or business that doesn't pay back or pay down its debt. I don't blame the takers of third world countries for taking funds from America. But to not use those funds for their intended purpose is a sham, and it wouldn't happen the second time for the same old sham on my watch believe me. However, our government officials have created money addicts. Those people, like drug addicts, are easy to control. Enough said? Our government might consider starting with having a few guidelines of self restraint when it comes to lending America's money to those that consider those loans more a gift than a helping hand. All loans have a responsibility tied to them. That would at least be a start to get on track with healthcare, to protect our borders, to stop the waste of our finances, to morally live up to the commitments to oaths of office, to show dignity and support to the elderly, to care for the homeless who, through no fault of their own, have lost their direction - why is it so hard to find our own sense of direction and depth as human beings when it comes to those who just need a hand up. When others are struggling to survive, why have we become so eager to want to control their lives if we happen to lend them a hand? Can't we just once lend a hand without controlling and expecting something in return OTHER THAN A THANK YOU AND AN HONEST WILLINGNESS TO TRY TO HELP THEMSELVES AND THEIR PEOPLE? I'm very much aware of reality and how cold and blunt it can be. But to deliberately harm and deprive another human of their most basic rights and dignity is a disgusting maneuver and is cancerous to the soul. What has happened to our basic sense of generosity? When used properly and responsibly it wouldn't take long until those down on their luck, through their own sense of pride and self reliance would want to return to the table to become productive citizens and proud responsible Americans. I can't think of any of the Presidents during my life time that had the natural ability to communicate this more than Presidents Kennedy and Reagan. No one had the natural power of persuasion and the charisma to move a nation forward more than Presidents Kennedy and Reagan. Not that all their policies were perfect or that they were perfect human beings, but that they had a natural calm and confidence and believability to do what was good for the entire nation. They had the ability to make you want to bring the best to the table. What we have today in our last three Presidents, Clinton, Bush, and BO, are slight-of-hand artists, shallow, egotistical, self-serving empty suits. Overall, they all have an air of untrustworthiness. But moreover, all are basically just unlikable people. Not one of them is presidential by any stretch of the imagination. None of them is believable or trustworthy when presenting the facts of their agenda to the American people. Bush's weapons of mass destruction have actually turned into BO's health care plan, and Clinton really doesn't even deserve a mention in my opinion. Bush wanted to circumvent the constitution, giving him unfettered control such as a dictator would want. To create illegal wars and to spy on Americans at will without the authority of the congress and his signing statement, the right to torture. BO is attempting to take control of private enterprise, financial institutions, health care, manipulate taxation, to penalize the productive citizens, eliminate your amendment rights and basically keep you enslaved until he can socialize this nation. Not going to happen in America bubbas - the American people will kick your ass. We are a free society and we will stay that way at all cost. You have never seen an uprising from a country as you will see when and if you attempt to enslave Americans by slowly eliminating their freedoms such as we are beginning to experience now as we watch the government bail out private enterprise with taxpayer money. American people are patient and open to a variety of proposals and are receptive to many different philosophies, but you will never take the constitution and bill of rights away from Americans. Those documents are our insurance policies. They are battle borne and purchased in full with the blood of real patriots. Those documents will be staying in tact, period! With all that is right with this country, there is still a lot that is wrong, and what better time to try and fix what's wrong than the present? There is a sense of unrest in this nation, and I can smell revolution in the air.

But if revolution is the last resort, then who better to lead the charge than the displaced residents and workers of the San Joaquin Valley in California? What better reason would one have than to protect what one has accomplished over a lifetime of work and sweat in developing a business, raising a family, and investing the remainder of everything you have in this country to become the 'bread basket of the world'. This is an accomplishment few can rival and is without a doubt, the pride of the nation. But just when you start to think that all is well with the world and you finally start to see light at the end of the tunnel, an abusive agency of the federal government, the EPA, sucker punches you along with everyone else by closing off the water that flows to the San Joaquin Valley. Water is the life's blood to your business and ultimately the survival of your family and friends. But because there happens to be a fish that is on the endangered species list, the delta smelt, that also thrives and whose habitat is located in the river that supplies water to the San Joaquin valley, the EPA doesn't have the gray matter to gather the fish, place them in hatcheries and transport some to a more suitable environment down river, or even other rivers, so that all can live and survive simultaneously. If you don't know about this dilemma facing the residents of the San Joaquin Valley, please give it some attention and investigation. It is a shame and actually criminal that the governor of the State of California who gets paid to think, to resolve, and actually govern the state, does nothing but give some lame excuse that he has contacted the President's office and requested that the President look into this matter. That is not governing anything. What is required here is action Mr. Terminator!!! But since your state is in debt in excess of $20 billion, it is doubtful, to me at least, that you are the man for the job, any job! As one resident spectator stated, "what is happening here, is the federal government is really going to do nothing but let this valley turn into a dust bowl, giving into the fact that the department of energy will probably confiscate the San Joaquin Valley through the process of Eminent Domain, and this rich valley will become a solar farm for the Department of Energy". If that is true, then it would appear that the Governor is in cahoots with the federal government on this issue and has orders to remain inactive. That really doesn't surprise me knowing the dark twisted minds of politicians. Politicians have been screwing the people over ever since the days of Caesar. If we do nothing, especially since we have been made aware, this kind of activity will continue. And we, the

American people, will once again be on the losing end. Can you say Flint, Michigan? Do we want this lush green productive location to end up like Flint, Michigan - all the muscle cut out and an empty helpless frame left to dry up and disappear? We all have a stake in what happens to each other. America doesn't act this way. Maybe other countries would displace their population for an opportunity for their own advancement, but not here in America. Not with the people of America. But let's leave this for a moment and turn our attention to B.O., and what he's doing for America today, right now, and let's find out just what his priorities are for the present time.

Let's see, there is a war raging in Afghanistan, and we're still involved in an illegal war in Iraq. We have a crisis in America with our economy. There is a rush to stop global warming, which is by all scientific studies other than Al Gore's, a farce. Our postal system is headed for bankruptcy. Our currency is weaker today than at any time in American history. We are in debt to Communist China in the trillions of dollars, and on October 1, 2009, the empire state building celebrated the 60 years of communist rule in

China. Our Commanding General in Afghanistan is screaming for help, while B.O. scoots off to Denmark to try and secure the World Olympic Games for Chicago, but was unable to even pull that off. Never mind the fact that 263,000 jobs just left America for foreign markets, in October 2009, our national percentage average of unemployment rate just hit 9.8%. But I will say this for B.O., he is consistent at least of one thing, and that is he has accomplished absolutely nothing but to embarrass the whole of America over and over including even those that like him. Why wouldn't he have a job czar, or an employment czar? He has this useless stall of tax paid stupid czars, and yet with all the assistants and cabinet members at his beck and call, he has only been able to pull off one thing, and that was go to Martha's Vineyard for a few days of vacation. Oh, I'm not discounting the fact that we all need to take vacations after a year of dedication to our jobs, but at least we get the job done before we take our vacations. It is not enough to march in protest any longer. But people who do march, and those who go on hunger strikes and set themselves on fire in protest to government's actions, or in-actions, only express how stupid they are or can be and accomplish nothing but bringing condemnation to the rest of the population. The opposition looks at you and wonders if everyone else in your class or association is as stupid as you. The days of Gandhi are over people! You are losing every chance of ever hoping to conquer your enemy, the government. The only thing any government will ever respect is power and force. And I'm not talking about everyone emailing their limp wrist representatives with comments regarding something of no interest to anyone. I'm talking of nailing their asses to the wall for failing to pay attention to the concerns about which you have been addressing. Remember this - THE RULER THAT DOES NOT LISTEN TO THE WISHES AND DEMANDS OF THE PEOPLE, IS NOT FIT TO RULE. Let this simmer for a while until you get the full impact of its meaning. Sixty-eight percent of the American people do not want government-run health care, but this government is telling you that they don't give a damn what you want, it's what the government wants. What this government has forgotten is that we have the right to revolt and the obligation to do so when necessary. We have a legal right to secede from this federal government, and the right to establish a new

government.   Ronald   Reagan   said,
"Government is the enemy of the people".
General George Patton once expressed, "No one
ever did his country a favor by getting killed by
the enemy". I'm saying you take your enemy
out.   You let your enemy know without
hesitation who is in control of the battle and
who is superior, that's what winners do. I'm
not going to be a loser. I hate bullies. The
people of this country have been on the losing
end for too long.   We have watched this
government   diminish   our   liberties,   our
freedoms, and our constitutional rights while
slamming the door to justice closed in our faces
as if our concerns and grievances mean nothing.
It is time to let them know that we know how
and what it takes to make a difference. You can
no longer sit on the sidelines and expect
someone else to carry the ball across the line for
the score. Those days are gone. You have a
responsibility to fight for change. You have a
commitment to your fellow men and women.
You have a responsibility to all American
citizens as they have to you. When you start to
realize that we're all in this together and that we
have to come together to free America from
bondage, you will then realize how powerful we
are as a body of over 300,000,000 strong. Free

her from of her captors. Get in the trenches and dig down for the duration because this government has no intention of letting you have your Constitution back without a fight. They have violated our rights granted under the Constitution. As Bob Shultz of We the People Foundation points out, the following seven items are violations of our constitution: 1) The Federal Reserve, 2) The U. S. Patriot Act, 3) The invasion of Iraq, 4) Undocumented illegal aliens, 5) The North American Union, 6) Gun Control, 7) The Federal Income Tax, as enforced by the IRS. So, who will defend the constitution? It sure as hell won't be the government. They're too busy trying to destroy it. You can't take a constitutional right and convert it into a crime as our government is attempting to do through the IRS taxing system. When the 16th amendment clearly states differently, also let me insert here, Article #299 from the original intent commentaries, We the People hearings, admit that the American people do not have to tolerate an income tax system in which the federal government requires a citizen to give up any constitutional rights. That pretty much tells it like it is. So who are you afraid of? Once again, if you do not understand that last paragraph or want

232

further information, go to the website, www.originalintent.com, and click on the commentaries link, or the hearing link. Now in conclusion, let me give you a few web listings that I think will be of help to you. Just start with www.dailybail.com for a treasure trove of information, both written and visual, you can spend hours at this site viewing and listening to the information you will need in doing research or just for your own collection of information. Next, go to www.nontaxpayer.org. The information that I am passing along to you will instill in you the courage to pursue the truth and alert you to the fact that government has been hiding from you what you have a right to know to protect yourself from fraud imposed on you by a bogus tax system, a fraudulent Federal Reserve System enforced by the department of justice and upheld in the courts by crooked judges. How convenient, huh? Next, visit the website www.wethepeoplefoundation.org. That site will confirm how many people just like you are racing down the same path to rediscover their rights that have slowly been eroded and thought to be lost. But a freedom loving people will not be deprived of their God-given rights by some less than human organization called the Federal Government. There are numerous websites that are available to you if you will just search for them, but the ones I am providing you are quick to go to the heart of the matter and quick to get you excited about the discoveries you are making. The biblical phrase "when you know the truth, the truth will set you free", could not have more meaning than it does within the context of what I have discovered in doing my research for this book. I would be remiss if I failed to share this with you because I know a great deal of you have lost interest in this government, and with good cause. But I also know the flame that burns for freedom never really dies. It just waits to be rekindled by those who burn a little hotter.

There are 535 politicians on the Capitol Hill Team, and there are 308,619,716 on the U.S. Citizens Team. Have no fear!

Next I want to give you a list of books that I find to be absolutely eye opening and stimulating. These books were a supply line of information in the writing of this book that all helped to give me direction. Throughout the writing this book I would pause to refresh my focus, and I would do so by selecting subject matter that was congruent to what I thought relative to my own belief. Also note that the book titles listed below are not in order according to my reading:

1. "The Committee of Three Hundred" by Dr. John Coleman
2. "The Creature from Jekyll Island" by G. Edward Griffin
3. "Secrets of the Temple" by William Greider
4. "Free Lunch" by David Cay Johnston
5. "The Dark Side" by Jane Mayer
6. "Mandate for Leadership" published by The Heritage Foundation
7. "Lost Rights" by James Bovard
8. "Liberty Nor Safety" by Robert Higgs
9. "The Revolution" by Congressman Ron Paul
10. "Man Hunt" by James L. Swanson
11. "Where Have All the Leaders Gone" by Lee Iacocca
12. "The Power to Destroy" by Senator William V. Roth and William H. Nixon
13. "Somebody's Gotta Say It" by Neal Boorts
14. "Fleeced" by Dick Morris & Eileen McGann
15. "The Federal Mafia" by Irwin Shiff Freedom Books

16. "The End of America" by Naomi Wolf
17. "Donkey Cons" by Lynn Vincent & Robert Stacy McCain
18. "Men in Black" by Mark R. Levin
19. "Liberty and Tyranny" by Mark R. Levin
20. "Crossing the Rubicon by Michael C. Ruppert
21. "Constitution in Exile" by Judge Andrew P. Napolitano
22. "The Flat Tax Revolution" by Steve Forbes
23. "The Fair Tax Book" by Neal Boortz & Congressman John Linder
24. "CIA, Inc." by F.W. Rustmann
25. "Cronies" by Robert Brice
26. "State of Emergency" by Patrick Buchanan
27. "Common Sense" by Glenn Beck
28. "American Government" by Nick Ragone
29. "Culture of Corruption" by Michelle Malkin
30. "Day of Deceit, The Truth About FDR and Pearl Harbor" by Robert B. Stinnett
31. "The End of America" by Naomi Wolf
32. The US Constitution and The Bill of Rights

Now, I will leave you with this one question to ponder. But before you answer, be sure that you're up to the task. How many of you are willing to join in a nationally organized class action suit against the Federal Government to force them to come to the table and respond to the peoples' demand for REDRESS OF GRIEVANCES?

As you are aware by now I'm sure, the people, the citizens of this great country, have the right to change and control this government - to seize all government property and install a government that serves the will of the people. Are you still there?

To order multiple copies of this book for your private use or for organizational use, go to **www.OutragedTheBook.com**.
Please email any comments or responses by clicking on the link provided at the website. We will go from there.